Breaking the **_
A prequel to The Unwanted Wife

the ungracious daughter

To Kent & Catherine

Sandy Maeck xoxo

SANDY MAECK

Disclaimer

The Ungracious Daughter shares the writer's firsthand experiences and a lifetime of observations, discussions, research, and education, coupled with experiences from other survivors. Although some facts, references to culture, customs, and traditions may be based on actual events, names and dates have been deliberately left out for legal and privacy reasons. It is the right of every victim to identify themselves when and if they choose to do so and their courage should be respected. Unless otherwise indicated, all names, characters, businesses, places, events, and incidents in this book are either the product of the author's imagination or used in a fictitious manner. Any resemblance to actual persons living or dead, or actual events, is purely coincidental.

Dedication

This book is dedicated to all the women, men, girls, and boys who have been abused, or lived through a traumatic experience, and is afraid to speak up because of shame, guilt, or feeling hopeless and lost. In reading this book, the reader will understand why I have chosen to step up and tell this story, to speak up, shout out and be the voice of millions of others who are unable to put into words the depth and breadth of their suffering. Like Maya, the main character in **The Ungracious Daughter**, I too went through similar traumatic experiences and I tell this story, not because it is unique, but because it is the story of so many others like me.

   - Sandy Maeck, Author

To my Family
This book is also dedicated to my beautiful children and grandchildren, and my wonderful loving husband. Thank you for always being so supportive and understanding, without which I would not be writing.

"Fiction is getting the truth told. It is a belief that is false but is often held to be true."

   – Sandy Maeck

Testimonials

I am proud of my mother for writing this story, experienced by so many women, men, girls, and boys, who keep their trauma hidden. These secrets and hidden trauma keep them in a loop of their past. They continue to be a people pleaser. This book will encourage those survivors never to extend themselves to others or stay places longer than they must. This book will allow your inner child to scream "Finally, someone loves me!"

   - Shauntelle Sims, Daughter

I see the love that surrounded me, the countless sleepless nights. The scraped knees and hurt feelings, your hugs and kisses magically made me right. Your sound advice and guidance when I needed you the most. Happy days spent together, talking and laughing as we still do. Now I know that many tmes you've gone without to build a better life for your children. Your endless love has made a difference in who we all are today.

Mom, your love has come full circle, as now I love and honor you. I love and respect you, for all you are and all that you do.

   - Shevaun Ramdin, Daughter

My mom and I have had the best relationship ever since I can remember. She's a loving, caring, best mother to me and my siblings. She has raised us singlehandedly and I'm so proud of her and what she has accomplished and for finally finding true love. Most of all I am proud of her for bringing awareness of abuse to a community that needs this to a great extent. I wish her only the best always.

   - *Kevin Shah, Son*

Sandy Maeck brings the true meaning of her name to life in her writing- "Brilliance"! Her courage to share her journey of trials and tribulations has broken an unspoken generational barrier that has allowed women, especially in the Caribbean diaspora, to finally break free from the emotional shackles of mental, physical, emotional, and sexual abuse. She has given them a voice to heal and not feel alienated. She empowers you to take that step and be free.

   Vashtie Doorga
   Shuga Magazine
   Doorga Entertainment

Sandy Maeck is a very dedicated hard-working person with lots of passion for her dance school and her students, whom she loves as her own children. Sandy founded her dance school twenty-five years ago, amidst all her difficulties and sufferings, and STCC is now one of the top dance schools in the Indo-Caribbean community in Toronto. Sandy is very ambitious and dedicated in anything she does, especially in making exemplary goals for herself. I am proud of her accomplishments and her ongoing support and guidance to my daughters.

   - *A proud dance mom, Annmarie Maharaj*

Sandy is an accomplished author who's also one of my favorites. In addition, she is a life and health coach and offers her knowledge to those who need it. After reading her first book, Sandy's portrayal of the characters was endemic to life in a certain culture and an environment of an era gone by. A delightful, albeit convoluted reading experienced by an extraordinary person.

- Robin Tiwari

First published by Ultimate World Publishing 2023
Copyright © 2023 Sandy Maeck

ISBN

Paperback: 978-1-922828-99-6
Ebook: 978-1-922982-00-1

Sandy Maeck has asserted her rights under the Copyright, Designs and Patents Act 1988 to be identified as the author of this work. The information in this book is based on the author's experiences and opinions. The publisher specifically disclaims responsibility for any adverse consequences which may result from use of the information contained herein. Permission to use information has been sought by the author. Any breaches will be rectified in further editions of the book.

All rights reserved. No part of this publication may be reproduced, stored in or introduced into a retrieval system, or transmitted in any form, or by any means (electronic, mechanical, photocopying, recording or otherwise) without the prior written permission of the author. Any person who does any unauthorized act in relation to this publication may be liable to criminal prosecution and civil claims for damages. Enquiries should be made through the publisher.

Cover design: Ultimate World Publishing
Layout and typesetting: Ultimate World Publishing
Editor: Maddie Johnson

Ultimate World Publishing
Diamond Creek,
Victoria Australia 3089
www.writeabook.com.au

Contents

Disclaimer	iii
Dedication	v
Testimonials	vii
Chapter One: Endearing	1
Chapter Two: This is Us	11
Chapter Three: The Miscreant	27
Chapter Four: The Contriving	33
Chapter Five: Vanishing Act	49
Chapter Six: Arresting Development	65
Chapter Seven: Disloyalty	71
Chapter Eight: The Executioner	79
Chapter Nine: Missing in Action	95
Chapter Ten: Unexpected Encounter	101
Chapter Eleven: Illegal Alien	109
Chapter Twelve: The Rogue	121
Chapter Thirteen: Living My Best Life	131
About the Author	137

Chapter One

Endearing

The sunroom was warm and clean, the floor-length windows were slightly open. It was a sizzling summer day, but every so often, a cool breeze brushes softly against Maya's face, making it comfortable to work in the sunroom.

On the sideboard behind her were two tall glasses, ginger tonic water, Bombay Sapphire gin, and fresh ice cubes in the ice bucket. Maya was waiting for Scott to come home from work. She had spent the night before at his house and worked from his home that day.

Now and again, she would glance up at the clock, but without anxiety. Merely to please herself with the thought that each minute gone by made it nearer to the time when he would come home. Nearer for her to tell him the truth. She was not nervous about this anymore. She had made up her mind. She knew that she had to do this for their relationship to move forward. He was the only one she ever felt comfortable and trusted to tell the truth. In her entire life, in all her relationships, she never felt that she could have shared this before.

There was a slow smiling air about her and about everything she did. The drop of her head as she bent over her laptop was curiously tranquil. Her skin, from the warmth of the summer, had acquired a wonderful glow, her mouth was soft, and her eyes, with their new peaceful calmness, seemed larger and brighter than ever before.

When the clock said ten minutes to six, she began to listen, and a few moments later, punctual as always, she heard the tires on the driveway outside, and then the car door slamming, footsteps passing the side door, the key turning in the lock. She put aside her laptop and stood up, and went forward to kiss him as he came in.
"Hello Babe," she said.
"Hullo beautiful," he drawled in his sexy accent.

Although Scott is German, Maya always thought his accent sounded more like a southern Ontario accent. He thought that was funny. His suit was sharp-looking and well-fitted. Exactly the sort of thing that a woman would pick out for her man to wear to work. That was something that had made her a bit nervous a few weeks ago, as she went suit shopping with him. She was not ready for this so early in the relationship. He had just gotten a promotion at work as the Project Service Manager, Nuclear Division. They had shopped for several suits, shirts, and ties. This one fit well, it made him look very handsome, and when he smiled as he took off the suit jacket, it felt magical.

She took the jacket and placed it on the back of the couch. Then she walked over and made the drinks, the strongest one for him, and a weak one for herself; and soon she was back again in her chair with the laptop, and Scott in the leather couch, opposite, holding the tall glass with both hands, rocking it so the ice cubes clinked against the side.

For her, this was always a blissful time of day. She knew he didn't want to speak much until the first drink was finished, and she was content

Endearing

to sit quietly, enjoying his company after the long hours alone in the house. She loved to luxuriate in the presence of this man and to feel almost like a sunbather feels, that warm male spark he radiates when they are alone together. She loved him for the way he sat loosely in a chair, for the way he came in a door or moved slowly across the room with long strides. She loved the intent, far look in his eyes when they rested in her, the sexy shape of his mouth, and especially the way he remained silent about his tiredness, sitting still until the gin had taken some of it away.
"Tired babe?"
"Yes," he said. "I'm tired,"

She paused a moment, leaning forward in the chair, she was about to get him another.
"You sit down Babe," he said "I'll get it!"
When he came back, she noticed that the new drink was dark amber, it must have a Balvenie Triple cask in it. His favorite whiskey.
She watched him as he began to sip the dark yellow drink, and she knew that she needed to get the conversation started.
If she waited, she would backtrack and 'chicken out.'
"Babe," she said. "Would you like me to get you some cheese? I haven't made any supper because it's Thursday and I thought we'd do the usual Thursday night thing – wing night? "
"Sure," he said.
"If you're too tired to eat out," she went on, "it's still not too late. There's plenty of meat and stuff in the freezer, and we can have it right here in the sunroom. And since we don't have work tomorrow, we can spend the time making a nice dinner together."
Her eyes wait on him for an answer. He smiles.
"I'll get you some cheese and crackers first." He spoke.
"I don't want," she said.
She moved uneasily in her chair, her large eyes still watching his face.
"But you must eat! I'll fix it anyway, and then you can have it, or not if you like." He continued.
She stood up and placed her laptop on the table by the lamp.

After years of research and having been in a number of unhealthy relationships, Maya knew it was difficult talking to a romantic partner about sexual abuse. It can be difficult regardless of whether the abuse happened recently or decades in the past, and whether you just started dating or have been together for many years.

Maya knew that although she did not ever have to tell her romantic partner about sexual assault, she knew that if she was going to have a comfortable and open relationship and be sexually intimate with Scott, telling him would help them both to understand what she was comfortable sexually with, and anything she might want to avoid because of her horrible past experiences.

She may end up having strong emotions or flashbacks during sex, and it would be helpful for Scott to know how she feels, and she would like him to support her during these times.

Since meeting Scott, she felt that trust, belief, and support from him and yet, she was unsure how to bring it up. Maya knew it was important that Scott knew about relevant things that happened in her past. She had already disclosed her abuse in her marriages and relationships but revealing her childhood traumas were still very painful to talk about. Yet, she knew that the more Scott knew, the better he would understand what she has been through and what may trigger her.

"Sit down," she said. "Just for a minute, sit down."
"Scott," she continued. "I've got something to tell you. There's no right time, no right place to tell you this so now is going to be that time, so here goes." She inhaled deeply and slowly exhaled.
It wasn't until then that she began to get nervous. But she knew she had to do this. He had to know the truth about her. He had already heard about Jason, Rahul, and Dinesh, but he needed to know. He needed to know these secrets that she kept so very long, buried deep within.
"Go on," he said.

Endearing

Scott lowered himself back slowly into the leather couch, watching her all the time with those strikingly blue bewildered eyes. He had finished the second drink and was staring down at her, frowning.

"What is it, Babe? What's the matter?" he said.
Maya had now become motionless, and she kept her head down so that the light from the sunset fell across the upper part of her face, leaving her chin and mouth in shadow.
"This is going to be a bit of a shock to you, I'm afraid," she said. "But I've decided that before our relationship gets more serious than it already is, I will tell you right away. After I tell you, you can choose to stay with me, or it would be your chance to walk away."
"I told you weeks after we met that there is no turning back, you are stuck with me for life," He smiled at her lovingly.
She went over and kissed him, his strong muscular arm immediately draping over her slight shoulders. She looked up at him and smiled weakly.
"Go on," He urged lovingly.
And she told him.

Maya knew that she was falling in love with Scott. But even though he had told her that he loved her, she could not bring herself to say the "L" word. She knew that she had to tell Scott about them. About her, her family, and their secrets. Maya had not confided in her past partners before, but she knew she loved Scott, and for this relationship to work, he had to know the truth.

"Ok. Here we go," she took a deep breath and it flowed, the words, the emotions, the pent-up frustration, and the anger. It all came out. Maya told him so much that night.

I am old enough now to know that there are very few women my age that have not been subjected to some form of sexual assault, and I know this because I am one of them. What I didn't know was that I could say no.

"We grew up in a small village called Kitty, in Georgetown, Guyana. Our family was a typical traditional Indian family. We were religious and very musically inclined. For nearly a century, the Maraj family name was well-known within the high society's powerful socialites. Our very large, close-knit family on my dad's side was always celebrating an occasion, singing, dancing, and having a merry time. Because my mom and dad, his brother, and my mother's sister had a double wedding, the two families were always celebrating together."

"Remember I told you my mom and her sister got married to my dad and his brother?"
"Yes, I remember, and I met your 'very large family' at Sandy's wedding in Long Island," Scott teased.

Maya smiled and continued.

"These occasions were an opportunity for my uncle, Khalil, to prey on his innocent young victim. What I have to tell you is about how my uncle sexually abused me for years."
She paused and looked at Scott to see his reaction. His face was drawn. She continued.

"This is about all the times he chose his moments, found me alone or asleep and put his hands in my panties, and felt me. All the time, he would ensure that I slept beside him so that in the middle of the night, he could push his horrible, clammy fingers into my small childlike vagina. This is about all the times he'd ask me to give him a peck on the cheek and then hold my face and push his tongue in my mouth. He said he loved me. I understood much later what this 'love' actually meant.

My earliest memories of my uncle's depravity seem rather innocuous in comparison to his later acts of evilness. He was always looking for an excuse to hug and kiss me. He often wanted me to sit on his lap. I remember when Nadia and I stayed at my grandparents. My dad went to Canada for a few months, and we had to stay there to go to school. My grandparents owned a pharmacy and sometimes my uncles would have to mind the shop.

Endearing

One particular day, I was asked to stay and watch the shop with Khalil, while Nadia and Grandma Betsy went to the market. He had put me playfully on his lap, offering candies, then he started to caress my arm, legs, and then my chest. I had just started to develop breasts. Then his hands were in my panties. That was the first time, at least that is when I can recall. Who knows if it was happening before that, I can't remember. That day was saved by a customer coming into the shop, but I was not always so lucky. That horrible nightmare went on for years and years.

Many times, Nadia and I were left alone with my uncle. One time, my grandparents had gone to a funeral. I can clearly recall it was a hot afternoon when my uncle asked me to come to his room. He was reading and said he wanted to show me something. I went inside and stood next to him. He got up to close the door and came back. He asked me to unbutton my pants. As I did that, he made me take them off and lie on the bed.

He went away, I thought he has gone, so I got dressed and was just about to leave when he returned. He had gone to get some oil. He again made me take off my pants and other clothes as well. He did the same to himself and applied the oil to his penis. I didn't even understand what was happening. He started touching himself, as he fingered me repeatedly. After he was done, he ejaculated on me, which I earlier thought was pee.

I got dressed and left. He asked me to never tell this to anyone and he will give me chocolates that my other uncle had brought from England. To this day I hate those chocolates.

The second time it happened was just a couple of days later. I believe he was drunk this time. It was a Saturday afternoon. I was drawing in my book and Nadia doing homework when he came to our room. He asked me to follow him to his room and my sister to continue with her homework. I had to oblige; I didn't have an option. There was no one I could tell. I went to his room, and the same thing happened again, and it wasn't the last time either.

During that stay with my grandparents, this assault continued repeatedly. Once, when I was asleep at night, he lay next to me and started kissing me and running his hands over my body. He started touching my vagina, then he made me touch his genitals. Then he ejaculated on my tiny hands. And at that very moment there was a power cut (blackout), and I was saved as my grandfather was coming up the stairs to see if we were okay.

Another occasion still leaves a very bad taste in my mouth. I was about eight years old. We went to my grandparents' house for dinner and to watch Uncle Randy's work of art, as he called it. You may also remember Uncle Randy from Sandy's wedding last month. I know it was a lot of people you met and may not remember everyone. He is my mother's third brother."

Scott nodded. "I remember. He was teaching me to dance "coolie bai" dance."
"Yes, that is right, he is the jovial uncle, always joking and making everyone happy," Maya continued with a weak smile, trying not to get sidetracked by the good memories of Sandy's beautiful wedding.
"Although Uncle Randy worked as a pharmacist, he was a fanatic about photography. This was his big hobby, and he had already spent a small fortune on photography equipment.

He was always taking everyone's pictures. He had just bought a new projector and invited the family to watch a slideshow of all the pictures he had taken over the years of the family. Everyone was so excited to watch a homemade family movie. My grandma had made delicious Dhal, rice, and chicken curry. After dinner, Uncle Randy turned off all the lights, and the house was thrown into darkness.

I remember everyone was scrambling to get a good seat. Uncle Randy was hanging a white sheet over the wall by the grandfather clock that stood majestically in the living room. Everyone was just about ready. But I was not ready. I did not find a proper seat; I was too busy trying to avoid Uncle Khalil. I began to panic and to my utter dismay, he grabbed me and lifted me onto his lap.

Endearing

'Here, you come to sit with me, it's the best view by the window,' I remembered him saying. His breath was close to my ear, still smelling of the curry. A toothpick in his mouth. I remembered that his desk was near the window overlooking the roundabout stairs and only one person could fit on the chair with it jammed up to the desk. It was the perfect spot for his dirty deeds. Sadly, I don't remember even seeing the movie.

Even at such a young age, I knew no one would find out that he was a predator.

No one seems to notice the signs that he was spending a lot of alone time with me, kissing and touching me inappropriately. The adults did not protect me, they didn't seem to notice that he was too eager to spend alone time with me, no one was cautious, and they left me alone with him so many times.

Khalil knew that because I was a girl, like my sisters, my dad didn't pay much attention to us. It is typical in Indian tradition. That was my mom's job because we were girls. I always resented how Bali paid more attention to his nephews," Maya continued sadly.

"Khalil had the perfect opportunity to take advantage of me. And I felt like it was my fault like I deserved this because mom and daddy loved Khalil, he was their favorite. I felt stifled, like a prisoner, which cannot escape from a box that I cannot get out of, and I had to accept it. I remembered how he put me on his lap as everyone settled in to watch the slideshow. As it got quiet, his dirty, clammy sweaty hands slowly crept up my dress into my little panties.

All this time as Maya spoke, she was curling the ends of her hair nervously as she spoke, not looking at Scott. She paused and looked up at Scott. His eyes were teary.
"It's okay Babe, go on, don't stop, you can tell me," He urged and took *a sip of his whiskey.*
Maya gulped down her gin in one quick mouthful.

"The abuse was sexual, and it was emotional. I could not tell my sisters or my mom, I couldn't tell anyone. I heard stories in the school of bad girls. They got sent to the Kali Temple, where the priest would beat them with neem leaves and branches soaked in turmeric and water. As a child, I believed this. Heck, I saw this with my own eyes. Now I know better. Now I know that this was just a form of worship for the fishermen's family. It was their beliefs.

However, this occurrence happens every year, up the street from us, in August. For nine days the local fisherman and his family held this ritual called the Kali puja. My cousin Mini and I would sneak over to our friends Diane's house to see the rituals because mom and daddy would not allow us - it was forbidden. Diane's house overlooks the fisherman's yard. We saw how the young girls got beaten. I thought if I ever said anything, I would end up there for them to beat the devil out of me. I was young, foolish, and naïve. So, Khalil continued his horrendous debilitating disgusting perverted act every opportunity he got."

Maya shifted in her chair and Scott could see she was uncomfortable talking about this. He took her small hands and squeezed them reassuringly.

"Mom was always working, busy with her teaching classes, her sewing classes, and her business. She was too tired and only wanted to relax. Daddy was always tinkering with his cars or in his garden or spending time with his nephews, teaching them to play table and dholak. I remember one time my mother was downstairs in her sewing room, teaching her students. He was upstairs with my sisters. Mom asked me to see if he needed lunch. I found him in my bedroom, taking off his clothes in a sexual way. I ran downstairs.

As a young Indian girl, unfortunately, I could not see or put together what was happening to me until I was about to write my common entrance exams.

Chapter Two

This is Us

Maya wanted Scott to know that meeting him had changed her and her children's lives so much, more than he knew. She was the happiest that she had ever been in her life, and she wanted Scott to know it was because of him.

"I had taken solitude in volunteering, writing, dancing, gardening, music, and painting, to keep me busy and get me through my past experiences, but I have not been able to talk about any of this with a partner before. I know that I need to do whatever makes me feel good, and get rid of the pain, the anger, the shame, the guilt, and the hurt that I have kept inside me for so long. I feel safe with you."

"You ARE safe with me, my love, I will protect you as long as I live, and there is no reason for you to feel those things any longer, you should not be the one to feel shame or guilt. That is for him to feel," Scott reassured her. Maya could see it in his eyes.

"Learning to love yourself after abuse can seem difficult, but it is completely possible," Scott said.
"I know. The love I give myself will go a long way in healing my wounds." Maya responded.

"I had, for a long time now, promised myself that I would never be in another narcissistic relationship. In the past, I have always gravitated toward this kind of relationship. My inner child was not letting me move away from that mindset and trust my intuition and I continued to attract distrustful people into my life. Anyway, I am getting ahead of my story. Let me go back too when I was able to talk about being sexually molested as a child."

When I finally told Mom, I was thirty-one years old, and it was right after I found out about Rahul's other wife and his betrayal and deceit. All I wanted was moral support from my family, from mom and dad, but they never asked what they could do to support me or what I needed …. All I wanted to hear from my mom was, 'are you Ok?' But it didn't happen. Nevertheless, I made myself a promise that I would no longer cover it up or keep it a secret. All those years, when I cried myself to sleep thinking I never did anything to deserve being abused, or times when I spent hours doubting myself. It never occurred to me that this was not my fault, and it was not my secret to keep. I often think about how many girls like me had their childhood taken away from them by perverts like Khalil, right where we thought we were the safest: in our own homes, or our grandparent's homes. I want to let other girls and women who were abused, just like me, know that this is not something that needs to be kept a secret any longer.

The shame is not on me, it's on him, my uncle, whom I stopped calling uncle a very long time ago. He lost that right, the day he laid his hands on me in an abusive way. I don't even call him by his name. I call him Zulu, but I don't remember why. The one who still smiles and cracks lewd jokes at family gatherings, with a drink in his hand. My uncle, without the slightest mark of guilt on his face. Oh, how I hate that face – that face that reminds me of a bad crook in the Bollywood movies. It irks me that he sleeps well at night with no sense of guilt, while I writhe and struggled all my life to find normalcy. No more! No more Scott, no more. That pervert will have to tell his family his secrets. I am not keeping his secrets for him anymore.

Maya had so much determination and strength in her voice now. Scott could see the pain and hurt still there, but also the courage and bravery.

"The shame is not on me. The guilt that churns my stomach is not for me to have. The secret is not for me to keep. Times have changed. I am setting myself free. I am not defined by those experiences. I am not broken. I am not the same child who spent years trying to find answers to questions that she should never have had to think about."

Scott smiled at her reassuringly, he did not want to interrupt her now. She needs this, she needs to let this out, to talk about it, to even be angry.

As Maya continued, Scott thought to himself. 'I wish this had never happened to this beautiful soul, but I am here now, to comfort and calm her when she goes to share the past and the worst time in her life.'

"It is taking a lot of courage to tell you this, I never told my ex or Sean's dad. I was too afraid, too ashamed, and too scared of the outcome."

"You know you can talk to me, you can trust me, and rest assured that I am here for you, always," Scott indicated lovingly.

Maya nodded. She knows that.

"And I understand. I understand that if this comes to light, and finds its way to my family, and my cousins, his daughters, it could wreak havoc on our family relationships. But I'm not telling this to hurt anyone or to create any havoc in my family. I'm telling this to bring light to this taboo topic in our community so that victims can become survivors and can tell stories without shame guilt, or fear, and most importantly, to get help.

The Ungracious Daughter

I am going off-topic here, but this is a story that is not only mine, but many other women like me, who are victims of sexual abuse. One in six women is abused by someone she trusts, someone she knows. Someone who should be protecting her instead of abusing her. I have heard many sad and horrific stories from women who have been or know someone who has been abused.

One such story haunts me to this day. My cousin Joanne had a friend in high school. Her name was Zameen. Joanne and Zameen were not very close, as Zameen was very shy and reserved. But Joanne continued to be her friend, despite her shyness and awkwardness. One day, Zameen never came back to school. Joanne always wondered what happened to Zameen, why and she didn't return to school. Many years later, Joanne got married and went to live in the Grand Caymans with her husband Dave. Joanne was very pleasantly surprised to meet her long-lost friend Zameen, who was living there for many years with her sister, her husband and her daughter. Her husband was working at the same company as Dave, and he had invited them for dinner. It was a very small community of Guyanese living in Grand Cayman and everyone knew each other or worked for the same company.

Joanne immediately inquired as to what happened and why she never returned to school. Zameen was evasive and changed the topic. Joanne sensed she wanted to talk about it but she was keeping it from her husband. Eventually, over the months, their friendship became stronger. One night they were having dinner together and after a few glasses of wine, Zameen confided in Joanne. Her story was out of a psychotic horror movie!

She did not return to school because she had become pregnant. What was most horrific was when she disclosed who the father was! She was pregnant with her father's child! Her daughter was actually her sister! Joanne could not believe her ears and thought, maybe Zameen was drunk. Or that she was telling a really sick and twisted joke. Sadly, it was no joke.

This is Us

Zameen's mother passed away when her dad was 44-years-old. Their 'perfect' life was shattered at 13 when her mother died. Zameen was so sad to lose her mother and felt lonely without her. They had always been such a tight pair together she was devastated at such a tragic lost. She had returned to school briefly and tried to settle back into normal everyday life, not talking about the passing of her mom or her loneliness to anyone. She quickly got used to being back home, but then started to notice a big change in her dad.

His looks seemed to linger a little longer on her than usual, which made her very uncomfortable. At the time Zameen wondered if he'd felt lonely without her mother, she couldn't shake the feeling that there was something sinister behind his stares. Her Dad and Zameen never had issues with being close before, but when he started requesting massages, she was very surprised. He'd never asked for them before, yet every day when she got home from school, he'd insist that she give his shoulders a rub.

He would complain of being achy from work. So, she would quietly oblige, pressing his shoulders awkwardly with her thumbs. To Zameen, it felt strange and wrong, but with only their dad at home, she didn't know what else to do but go along with it. She hoped massages would be the only unusual request, but things took a sickening turn when she came home from school one day and her dad started staring at her chest, commenting that her boobs were huge for a 13-year-old. Then he suddenly started groping her breasts. She was frozen, stunned, and prayed it would be the end of it. But it was like a switch had been flicked inside her dad and that night he raped her for the first time. She remembers feelings of hopelessness as she struggled beneath his heavy body, powerless to move. How she cried for her mum and siblings, but nobody was there to help. She prayed it would be a one-off but after that first time, it seemed her dad was hungry for more.

He ramped up his abuse until he was raping her every day, with no one at home to get in the way. She had never felt so scared and alone. The abuse went on for two years as she lived in fear of her dad's horrifying attacks. She learned to close her eyes to try and blank out what he was doing but every night, as she lay in bed afterward, she hoped that it was the last time he'd hurt her. He raped her several times over the period and then Zameen got pregnant!

He then started his horrible attacks on his second daughter, Zameen's twin sister Zubeida. On one occasion he also raped her in his car. This continued for months, with both girls being raped several times a month. Then his attention turned to his youngest daughter Zeila. The first time he raped her was in a room in Georgetown hotel, when he took her shopping that day. Their father used to threaten his daughters and even make them swear on the Quran not to reveal anything.

It was only when Zubeida also got pregnant, that the daughters spoke to their mother's sister. Zameen remembered how she wanted to kill him after Zubeida told her that she thought she was pregnant.

They both held each other and cried. They decided to tell their mom's younger sister. They sobbed the whole way to their aunt's house, just wanting to run away from everything.

Their aunt was shocked as she opened the door to their tear-stricken faces and demanded to know what had happened.

Everything came spilling out and it was agony as they finally spoke of the pain they had lived through for so long in silence. In dismay, they soon discovered that she too had shared the same experience at the hands of their dad.

What was most horrendous was when she told them that their mother had been raped too, and she actually had a heart attack while being raped by their dad! None of this was ever disclosed. The girls and their aunt decided to make an escape plan and they started growing tomatoes and eggplants and selling them to the neighbors. Their aunt secretly started cleaning homes to help them to save money to escape.

This is Us

One night when the father was getting drunk at the bar, they left. To their horror, their aunt refused to leave. She was too afraid. They never looked back and never knew what happened to their aunt. Zubeida now lives in New York with her daughter. She never married.

This is the most horrific and disturbing story that I have ever heard, and it is haunting me to this day.

Scott was appalled to hear such a devastating tale and felt sick to his stomach. He had to get some fresh air.

"Let's go for a drive," he suggested to Maya.

"Yes, that would be a nice break," Maya took a deep breath.

"I would like you to continue your story though, you need to get this out, and you are suffering from all this bottled-up negative energy," Scott continued. "We can take a blanket, some wine and cheese and go by the lakefront."

"That sounds lovely," Maya agreed.

The drive to the lakefront was only 10 minutes away. The Ajax waterfront is one of their favorite places to sit and have a glass of wine. It is a gem of unspoiled beauty kilometers of park land spanning the Town's southern border, along the shores of Lake Ontario.

They took their drinks and walked to the edge of the rocks to watch the sun sink toward the lake. Waves pounding the rock mercilessly. The surface of the lake was like a thousand shades of gray and silver, the spray was foamy and angry against the rocks, slick, oily. Their silhouettes slicing the surface of the water after every push and pull of the tide.

Maya shivered from the slight chill and leaned into the warmth of Scott's body. The moment felt incredibly intimate for her after the stress of her tales.

The Ungracious Daughter

Neither of them spoke. Even if they had, the salty winds would have swept their words away. Maya's mind was tired, and her nerves frayed. They sipped their drinks, and she left a tear rolling down her cheeks. Scott squeezed her as she cried. Scott noticed she was emotional but said nothing. The wind dried her teardrops as quickly as they fell and after a while, she laughed at herself and thought 'why am I crying, what is done is done, I am telling this story so that I can move on.'

They had dinner at Island Mix restaurant in Pickering. The Thursday night wing special was Scott's favorite. That evening he ordered the Caribbean jerk and Maya the Island Mix hot. They loved going here and the owner knew them well, and even came over to their table to have a shot of Bourbon with them.

After dinner, they drove back to the house and settled in on the couch in the TV room. Maya's head on Scott's chest, her hair spread across his arm, the light from the TV made her eyes twinkle in shades of hazel.

Maya continued her story, not wanting to leave out any details that she had mentally summarized.

"When I met Rahul, I mustered up the courage to confront Khalil. I traveled with Rahul to Trinidad to confront him. For weeks before we went there, I had everything prepared in my head about what I was going to say to him, and how I was going to confront him. I did not tell Rahul what I was going to do. I planned to get Khalil alone. It was daunting, to say the least. Sadly, when I met his wife and two beautiful young daughters, I could not bring myself to do it. I could not hurt them. They were so kind and wonderful to me and treated me so well. His daughters were so excited to see me, that I didn't have the heart to do that them. I was not ready to tell his secrets. This was the same visit to Trinidad where I met Rahul's mother and sisters. Now, that too was something I never was able to comprehend. They too were so welcoming, loving, kind, and generous and welcomed me as a daughter-in-law. They never once indicated that he was already married!

This is Us

Our visit was the week before the popular Trinidad Carnival. When we arrived at the airport in Trinidad we were greeted by the sound of a steelpan. We had breakfast right at the airport. Delicious doubles, a wonderful sloppy sandwich made with two pillowy soft baras, like flatbread, filled with Channa also known as curried chickpeas and mouth-watering condiments and Caribbean flavors. It was my first taste of what was an authentic Trinidad experience or what my Trini friends would say is the typical "TNT" experience."

Maya smiled at Scott, "Remind me to take you for Doubles, you will love it."
"Sounds delicious, any meat in it?"
"No Scott, not everything has to have meat," Maya laughed.

"It was intimidating meeting Rahul's family. We are both from different religions, which is, sadly, still a big deal in our culture. We are also from different countries, he is originally from Trinidad, me from Guyana. I already had been married and had three children. I did not know if they would appreciate that or even accept me. Rahul was not a traditional Muslim and did not follow the daily routines of a Muslim, but he would fast for Ramadhan and read Namaz throughout the holy months.

I was expecting some reservations from his family, but something unexpected happened, his mother and sisters immediately treated me like a daughter and a sister. The evening we arrived, Rahul's mother organized a dinner party at their home. All of the extended family would be there. I found out just as the jet lag was starting to hit me. I had to take a nap. When I woke, the house vibrated with the hum of activity and chutney music blaring from the stereo. I was bombarded by a tidal wave of unfamiliar faces — all staring at me with curiosity. Who was this girl that their cousin/nephew/grandson had brought from Canada? I was the first non-Hindu girl to join the family. Or so I believed.

My fight or flight response told me they were hungering to tear me apart. I wasn't one of them. On the surface, everyone was super nice. But I felt simultaneously on display and on trial. Everyone wanted my attention. Sisters, aunts, uncles, cousins — everyone had questions for me. I'm not sure how I got through the evening. At the end of it, we had enough follow-up dinner invitations at people's houses to pack the next two weeks. In Indian culture, when someone is visiting from abroad, it is customary to invite them over to your house for dinner. And it's mandatory for the guest to graciously accept, or risk creating a grievance which cannot be repaired. I got through it. And it wasn't nearly as bad as I thought.

I fell in love with Rahul's mom's house immediately. She lived in a beautiful pink and white three-story house on Waterloo Street, in Charipichaima. The house somehow looked like a little palace for a royal family. Natural light came in through the wrap-around veranda and the house was equipped with modern appliances and air-conditioning, which was a big relief to me as the temperatures were scorching hot, even at night. I loved the picturesque trees and tropical flowers plants around the entire house, it made it look so beautiful and tranquil.

Rahul and I had our own room on the third floor of the house. A maid was dispatched every morning to sweep, mop, dust, and shine. Rahul's relatives weren't out to get me as I imagined. They were just curious. They wanted to know all about me. Looking back, they probably thought I was a home wrecker. No wonder they all wanted to see me.

For the next two weeks, we managed to keep all the invitations and still tour the entire island. I have to tell you of the beautiful places we visited, and I hope one day you and I can visit this beautiful paradise. You have heard enough about Trinidad from my friends, so it probably comes as no surprise that the stunning tropical beaches took my breath away, especially since I was escaping the cold Canadian winter. The first place we visited was Maracas Beach, on the north coast of Trinidad. It's the most popular beach, although it's not that busy on a weekday. There is no shortage of rum-infused beverages, friendly people, and unspoiled beaches.

One memorable day trip was to Las Cuevas Beach. It involves a scenic drive along the coast, revealing some stunning views of the Caribbean Sea. It is an almost perfect beach, green lush surroundings, great waves, nice clean water and a small shop with Trini snacks, like bake n' shark and shrimp. The sunset was breathtaking. You would love it here Scott.

We also visited Nylon Pool, so named because of the transparency of the water, like nylons. It's an offshore sandbar, where you feel like you're wading in the middle of the ocean. Legend has it that it's a fountain of youth of sorts.

That week we also managed to hang out with all of Rahul's friends and family and we were 'liming by the river' many times during the week. I didn't know what 'liming by the river' meant at first but basically, it means hanging out by the river, cooking, eating, and drinking. We visited Mayaro Beach on the East Coast where I got good lessons on liming, as you might imagine. There are often some cold beverages involved but the focus here for me was taking in some of the gorgeous sceneries as well as great food and awesome company. It was a great vacation and an unforgettable one. After two weeks of lazy days, I was feeling rich and rejuvenated.

Alas, I did not get a chance to speak with Khalil before I left, but I also did not want to spoil that relaxed feeling.

By the time we returned home, I realized that I missed my time in Trinidad and never got a chance to confront Khalil.

I missed the outpouring of love, the care, and the solicitude. I missed the long, leisurely conversations with no agenda. The laughter at the silly jokes and the awkward childhood photos of Rahul. The days melted together with no shrill calendar reminders demanding that I return to work.

I was disappointed in myself for not confronting Khalil since the main purpose of the visit was to do so. I then decided to write him a letter, thinking it might heal me. I wrote a very angry letter to him, but then I didn't feel the need to send it.

I didn't write it for him. I wrote it to articulate to myself just how I felt and to validate my anger and my pain. I didn't need him for that. At the time, I believe that confrontation, even in the form of a letter, gave him too much power. Even if it didn't obligate me to hear any kind of a response, I didn't want to imply that I wanted to open a discussion. Now that I look back on it, I just didn't want to open those wounds. It was best left buried. But was it, though?

Maya looked up at Scott questioningly. Scott did not want to interrupt. She was not looking for an answer, just reassurance that she was allowed to continue.

After years of silence, I heard through my mom that his health wasn't very good and that he might die. I'll be honest. I wanted him to die. I wanted him to cease existing. I thought it would heal me. And then I thought of my mother. She loved him. It will pain her. I was very emotional. Then I felt guilty for wishing him dead. You would expect as a survivor, I would feel relief, maybe even happiness if he died. But his death would not mean the trauma would be over. I have never stopped processing the traumatic experiences. Every time something in my life changes, I have to reframe my perspective to fit the abuse back into a narrative that makes sense to me so that I can make peace with it again. I know that recovery is an endless cycle."

Maya emits a long, deep, audible breath expressing sadness.

"Scott, did you know that when someone leaves a mark on us as huge as sexual abuse, it stays in the survivor's minds, and unfortunately, the abuser has a bigger influence over us than we like to admit?

I had fantasized about killing him on so many occasions, dreamt it, joked about it, and threatened to do it when my anger bubbled over, but nothing had prepared me for the idea of him no longer existing in this world. The thing is, I wanted him to die on my terms. I wanted to have the power this time, to serve myself that appetizing slice of justice. In reality, I never would have had the opportunity to act out my revenge fantasies, they were simply a coping strategy and in dying on his terms, he took that away from me.

I also struggled to comprehend that someone so powerful who had ruled over me for so long could be reduced to a body on a slab in a morgue. Death would humanize Khalil in a way, and my mind would be forced to see him as a fallible, mortal human, requiring me to reframe everything he had put me through.

As sick and perverted as he was toward me, he was not only my sexual abuser—he also showed a lot of love and affection towards me and my sisters. And since my dad was not very affectionate, my mother's brothers were the closest thing to love from a male figure that we had. My dad was distant and did not show affection, but my uncle was very emotionally and physically affectionate. My mom's other brothers were not like Khalil, they had a genuine abundance of love, and hugs, for us. It was simply love for one's niece.

But Khalil pursued me for his gratification, and I was an emotionally starved child, I couldn't afford to be picky. He treated me as "special." To a child, it was a good feeling. I did not know any better.

I must have thought this was normal at the time. When we would go visit my grandparents, he would pick me up and throw me in the air. I was convinced I could fly like Mary Poppins. He was involved with his affection just like the other brothers, but he wanted gratification as well. Yes, he caused me enormous pain, but he was also one of the few people whom I felt any amount of connection with as a child. Though the comfort I got from him was mixed with fear, and the "love" I got from him carried the price of sexual compliance, that was as close to love as I ever had. I did not know any better. When I got older, I realized how wrong I was. How victimized I was, for as long as I could remember.

Now I must break this cycle. Will I be the ungracious daughter for telling the truth? For breaking the silence? For telling his secrets?"

The Ungracious Daughter

Maya looked up at Scott again, with questioning eyes.

"As you said, this is not your secret to keep," Scott replied, looking down at her face. This face that he had fallen in love with the moment they met. Scott was surprised at the connection that he and Maya had the first time they spoke on the phone but was thrown off by the instant spark they both felt when they met. There is no denying it or escaping. He was madly in love with Maya. He was determined to help her get through this.

As Maya continued, she could feel the emotional tension being released and with that came the tears.

"The responsibility of preserving this institution called family is not my burden. There are no consequences for me, there should only, always have been, consequences for him. Consequences he has never had to face. I am gifting myself freedom today from experiences that I had never signed up for."

Maya was clenching her teeth to stop herself from crying. Scott held her close, and she buried her head in his chest. When she finally looked up at Scott, it was for assurance that what she was saying was true.

"Babe, I am so sorry, so very sorry you had to go through all of this. I am at a loss for words. How can any man call himself a man and abuse an innocent child? I cannot comprehend this," Scott said angrily.

Now Scott realized why Maya grinds her teeth at night. Why she is so restless at night. Poor Maya. Scott's heart ached with pain for Maya's suffering.

"I know. I want to go on and continue telling you everything so that I can put it behind me. I want to bring it in the open so that it can help others to talk about their horrible experiences as well. I am hoping for a day when women do not have to talk about their abuse, in hushed whispers, or sharp breaths, between tears. I am hoping for a day when women can talk about it, knowing that people they trust and love, will have their backs. For women to be able to confront and hold their abusers accountable for their actions. I am hoping for a day when this never has to be spoken about because it no longer happens to women."

"That would be incredible! But whatever the case, remember, the shame is not on you, it's on him," Scott reassured her.

"From deep inside, I wanted to hear it was not my fault. I didn't do anything wrong; it was not my fault. I didn't go to him. He preyed on me, with every chance he got, he touched me in a place that he was not supposed to."

Maya was tired and drained. She wasn't sure how much more she can talk about this now. She felt emotionally exhausted. Her body felt the strains of the emotions.

Chapter Three

The Miscreant

The next day, Maya continued her story after breakfast. Scott was getting very good at making Guyanese food. That morning he made 'bhaighan choka,' a tasty dish of roasted mashed eggplant. It is traditionally made by roasting eggplant over a grill until it's charred and infused with smoky flavor, then scooping out the inside and mashing it with roasted peppers, tomatoes, onion, garlic, and butter. This is a delicious, flavorful, and creamy dish that's best served with paratha roti, a soft leafy flatbread. Maya made the Paratha, whilst Scott roasted the eggplants. This had become one of Scott's favorite dishes.

After Breakfast, they settled in the sunroom, Maya lying on the sofa, her head brazed up against Scott's chest. Her hair fell softly on his stomach. He caressed her face softly as she continued sharing her story.

Eventually, I plucked up the courage to tell my Grandma Betsy. It was more like "why did you let this happen to me?" Real grandmas take care of their grandchildren. Real grandmas are the ones who protect their grandchildren. Regrettably, like most victims, I found myself trapped long before I had become aware of any warning sign.

By the time I had the courage to talk about it, I had already left Jason. Grandma Betsy was closest to me then, staying with me for weeks and helping me take care of the children after I left. I did not want her to take any actions, I just wanted her to listen, believe me, and have compassion. After all these years of being afraid, I finally felt brave enough to tell her what happened. Surprisingly, she was very patient and considerate as I told her the details.

She was riddled with shock and then guilt. She was so sorry that she did not protect me. That weekend, when she went to his house, she confronted him. Of course, he profusely denied it and threatened to cut her off if she ever talked about it again. He told her that I was making up for my flaws and shortcomings by accusing him of such vile, despicable actions. Khalil, being a narcissist, only thought of himself. He is known to brag. He describes himself as intelligent, rich, modest, intuitive, and creative - but always excessively and extraordinarily so. Remember that abuse is a multifaceted phenomenon. It is a poisonous cocktail of control, conforming to social and cultural norms, and latent sadism. Khalil had control over me and his secrets all this time. He had conquered and overpowered me.

Now, suddenly, after all these years, he was losing all that control, that domination. He had to vanquish these "lies" as he called them. He had to remain the controller and "look good" or "save face" in front of the family. He made my Grandma Betsy promise not to talk about it anymore and convinced her that it was going to ruin the family. He told her that this family does not air its dirty laundry publicly, and the family's honor and repute must be preserved. He threatened her with words like 'what will your friends say? What if the people at your temple find out her lies? What will they think of you? If you tell anyone, and they inform the authorities, they will take me away and the whole family will disintegrate. You will have no place to live, and they will take all your money away too.'

It was never discussed again. The family's avoidance to talk about this or to even hold him accountable or responsible for what he had done, was just a defense mechanism.

And this same defense is what gives Khalil the power over me. By not bringing my abuse and exploitation to light, he continued to feed lies about the trauma."

"In all my years of unpacking hurtful memories, writing became my therapy. But I kept going back to the one thing that I felt the most anger about, and how they must have known, my mother, my father, my grandfather, all who love me so much. How did they not know? How did they let this happen to me? Why abuse a child? In all honesty, I do not even know when it started, I don't even remember. All I know is ever since I can remember, it was happening."

Maya was tearful as the words came. Scott was angry, angry that no one had the courage or valor to protect young Maya. All that pain and hurt she suffered as a child, must have been unbearable and agonizing for her.

Why did her family minimize her sexual trauma? Did they not know that it is one of the most invasive types of abuse that can single-handedly destroy someone's overall mental state and life? Did they not understand that Maya was robbed of her innocence, her childhood, and her peace of mind?

Scott suppressed his anger. He wanted Maya to continue. Inside, his blood boiled.

"I was afraid. There I was this little thing, a tiny person. And yet I was harmed by this horrible perpetrator."

Scott held Maya closer.

In the shelter where I stayed after leaving Jason, the counselor indicated that sexually abused girls are at a greater risk of entering into abusive relationships. Isn't that sad? They usually feel as though they don't belong in a healthy relationship. They do not know how to do that as their inner child is always telling them that they are unworthy.

Protecting his secret was put on me. He put that responsibility on me. My safety was up to me. I was a defenseless young child. I was not aware that I needed to protect myself from my uncle.

I always wondered why it was such a difficult task to discuss emotions and feelings about mental health, with Caribbean parents and grandparents. Emotions and feelings will never be discussed. How can I break down this experience and transgress how it impacted my life today? There is no greater isolation a child can suffer than that of incest. Without healing, that sense of isolation follows the survivor into adulthood.

At times I blamed my parents for permitting the abuse. Sometimes I believe they could have prevented it if they knew. I want to believe that my dad would have killed Khalil if he knew. I believe that deep in every abused child, lies some degree of blame for the parents. But they are not always at fault. It's very hard to figure out who should be blamed in addition to Khalil. Particularly since the abuse continued for years. Do I blame my parents, who continually left us at my grandparent's home, or do I blame my beloved Grandma Betsy who did not properly watch over us and put us to sleep in the same beds as our uncles when we stayed over? In my heart, I knew she thought nothing of this. She did not know how evil her son was. And it was just him, the others never laid a hand on me in that way. And the love I have for them probably runs deeper because of that.

Maya sighed and exhaled.

It makes it harder to talk about the abuse because I feel like I owe my parents so much for the years they took care of us in childhood and as a teenager. We were involved at the temple from a very young age. My parents worked so hard to provide a wonderful life for us. In the life we lived, none of our cousins had the same privilege.

The Miscreant

It seems ungrateful of me to criticize my parents or grandparents.

Yes, I owe them something for the life they provided.

Yet, it went on so long under their noses. I asked myself so many times 'Why didn't they know?"

Some called it neglectful abuse, which is a kind of psychological abuse. This is the hardest for me to understand and cope with because I get confused about whether it was done intentionally or not. But the truth is, it doesn't matter what the intention was because the results are on par with all other types. For years I ended up feeling like I wasn't worth paying attention to or worth loving. For years, I was unable to pinpoint the source of these feelings.

I stumbled through life feeling like a fraud and the successes that I did achieve, especially in school and then at work, didn't make me feel I was worthy. That feeling was so subtle, that I did not realize the source was unhappiness as a child. My parents said I cried every morning. Did they not want to know why I was so unhappy or the cause of my crying every morning? I wet my bed as a child until I was eight years old. They never bothered to find out why. They didn't notice their child was unhappy for all those years.

Years later, I still feel terrible for initially discussing the sexual abuse with my parents, because my true feelings on the matter might lead me to accuse my parents of neglect. Then they may get all upset and try to defend themselves, and my problems regarding the sexual abuse would be ignored until I would be forced to agree nothing was their fault. Then the outcry would drown out everything else! Eventually, the only person left to blame would be me! For not telling earlier!

Even now, thinking about the 'what if' leaves a lump in my throat. If I had enough attention from them, not only would it not have happened more than once, but I would also have trusted them enough to tell them a long time ago.

The Ungracious Daughter

I have so many conflicting thoughts on this. In one sense, I disagree and think it's wrong to place 100% of the blame on my parents for neglect because I don't think they are 100% to blame.

The next moment I want them to take the blame. Getting them to accept any blame, no matter how small, is a big step in their understanding of why it took so long for me to come forward and speak.

Don't get me wrong, I love them dearly and would do anything for them. You know that. I know that they are not perfect, and I do not shy away from letting them know I still love them, blame them or not. But my problems should not be neglected by them now that I am ready to speak.

Scott noticed that Maya was beginning to cry softly. She was distraught and looked traumatized. He held her close to him and pushed the hair gently away from her face. He knew she had to take a break from telling him about her horrible, hellish experience.

"Tomorrow is a holiday, and we have the rest of the weekend to talk about this. Take a break babe." Scott reassured her.
Maya took a deep breath and shook her head in agreement.
That night both Scott and Maya could not sleep and ended up cuddling and watching movies to get the thoughts of Maya's childhood out of their minds.

Chapter Four

The Contriving

The next morning Maya woke up, realizing that Scott had already gone downstairs. She stretched her legs off the bed and onto the floor, her arms raised to the ceiling in prayer, like any other day. She got out of bed and waltzed into the kitchen where she could smell the aroma of Scott's special blend of freshly brewed coffee. Scott was always up, bright and early, fixing breakfast for Maya.

But for some reason, this day didn't feel like every other. With all the emotion from the last few days talking about such disturbing details rushing through her head, she realized that she was deep in thought when she came to a halt in front of Scott, who was smiling at her absentmindedness, holding a cup of coffee for her. Scott made eggs, bacon, and pancakes and they had breakfast in the sunroom, their favorite place to eat in the mornings.

Later that day, they nestled down in the TV room. Maya lying on the sofa, her head curled up against Scott's chest.

The Ungracious Daughter

They sipped coffee and flipped the channels.

"So, did Khalil abuse any of your other sisters or cousins?" Scott suddenly asked.

Maya almost knocked over her coffee in shock. She looked at him as she fidgeted and shuffled uneasily in her seat. Scott knew her so well, even her thoughts. She was thinking the same thing. They always joked about their "morphic resonance" as they often find themselves saying or thinking the same thing at once.

"I always wondered that myself, because I always wondered if that was the reason why Rania acted the way she did towards my parents."
"What do you mean?" asked Scott.

When she met Veer, she changed so much. She became ungrateful, churlish, and unappreciative towards my parents. Her betrayal, deceit, and disloyalty left them embarrassed and ashamed for years. But I always wondered if it was because she too was abused by Khalil that that was her way of making my parents "pay" for what happened to her.

Maya used her fingers to make air parenthesis as she said the word "pay."

"So, she was the Ungracious Daughter?" Scott teased.

Maya laughed and took a sip of her coffee, enjoying the delightful aroma, "Maybe."
Then she thought of Rania. Sadly, Rania was never the person who talked to anyone about anything.

I know many people will say, "but you don't know if she was abused," and to a certain extent, that's true.

When we lived a short time together, I tried to broach the subject with her. I tried to let her know that no matter what happened, I am there for her, that I love her, and she can talk to me about anything, but it was hard, she did not open up at all. She never wanted to talk about the past, or about our childhood. She would simply walk out of the room when I tried to talk about it, even if I only wanted to talk about myself.

She never even wanted to talk about her awful husband. So, I ended up spending more time saying to her, "You are a strong woman," "You are so kind and so generous."

When a woman is being controlled or emotionally abused, one of the key weapons an abuser uses is to demoralize the person, so they feel they don't have the ability to tell the truth. I felt that was what happened to her. She is not as strong as I am, she is too weak, too vulnerable and she may never tell the truth.

Maybe that is why she became so resentful and aggrieved to this day. Resentment can cause one to hold on to things that hurt them, like burning pieces of wood, they can't seem to let go of. They do this to be able to throw those things back at their loved ones, who hurt them, anytime they please. The thing is that, by doing this, they only end up hurting themselves. There's nothing positive about holding onto that burning hatred and anger for so long.

Sometimes those who experience this deep and self-destructive feeling are people who didn't learn to forgive others. But this is a very complex subject that has many different nuances.

It doesn't matter what people say about this feeling. The truth is that it's quite universal and recurrent and that no one is exempt from feeling it. A person who experienced traumatizing events such as abandonment or betrayal is very prone to feeling resentment.

A lot of resentful people have been victims of complicated and hurtful situations where they didn't see any other way out than bottling everything up inside them as anger. But until we understand the reason behind this feeling, we might not understand it. Nonetheless, it's not a healthy feeling at all. I know, I have learned the hard way not to bottle up my anger. This can eventually cause health issues as well. When I was in university, I had to do a minor. I chose psychology. It was fascinating.

I wish I had known all of this when I was married to Jason, but it was not until after I left that I went back to school again. During that course, I learned that the first reason why bottling up anger isn't healthy is that it's characterized by a highly harmful fact, like chronicity. This is an anguishing state that tends to prolong over time, to the point where it can interfere with other aspects of a person's daily life. It's not uncommon for that person's mood to change. Also, it's not uncommon for them to stop trusting others, have sudden attitude changes, and mistreat others. Resentment is like rust. It spreads and ends up debilitating an entire structure and identity. She may have turned the pain into anger. That anger then leads to resentment or betrayal. Forgiving isn't the easiest thing to do. But we must keep in mind that it's an important thing to do if we want to get closure and move on with our lives. Resentful people don't want to forgive anyone. All they do is feed their pain by replaying the triggering events over and over.

But I learned that by doing this, the feelings of despair and anguish intensified.

"Wow, that is deep Maya," Scott replied.
"Yes, I always kept her betrayal a secret, but I am not sure why."
"Her betrayal?" Scott asked.
"I am not sure if is betrayal, disloyalty, or hurt, but it was pretty bad."

"You want to talk about ?" Scott asked.

"Yes, I do. There is so much that I need to let go of. Too many secrets, lies, and betrayals, treachery, perfidy, the list goes on. I need to get this out. I need to let go of all these untold truths. I need to break the silence. I have kept these secrets for far too long, but it's painful to talk about what hurts," Maya said.

"I know that everyone has secrets but holding on to secrets can be harmful. Even you may have secrets, Scott. If you're like most people,

The Contriving

you can probably count about a dozen pieces of personal information that you've never shared with anyone and probably never will."

"It could be that one-night stand with a stranger," Maya teased Scott. Scott laughed and planted a kiss on Maya's slender neck. "I can assure you that is not the case."
Maya smiled up at him but continued.

It doesn't have to be that extreme. Many people keep their political and religious views secret, especially when they believe no one else will agree with them. Some people hide finances, whether they have a lot more or a lot less than others think. Likewise, sexual orientation and sexual behaviors, in general, are private matters for most people. But keeping secrets can often be harmful in the long run, both physically and psychologically. It's not the withholding of information from others that hurts us. Instead, it's the fact that we tend to ruminate on our secrets.

Although, I feel that some secrets we keep don't hurt us, since they're nobody else's business anyway. But others weigh heavily on our minds, and these are the ones that harm us over time, especially a traumatic experience. So, letting it out and having clarity about the reason for keeping it a secret can reduce the psychological harm that comes from ruminating about it.

"I get it. Indeed, it is best to get it out if you are comfortable telling me. As you said secret-keeping affects one's mental health. Not only does the secret stress out the secret keeper, but it also acts as an indication and reminder that they're being inauthentic. Anything that a person feels guilty, ashamed, or uncomfortable about certainly has the potential to impact their mental well-being," Scott said.

"Do not punish yourself any longer. Let go, babe." Scott urged. "Keeping pent-up emotions and secrets inside can mentally affect you in other ways. I am sure you have exerted a great deal of effort to hide this secret, which may come at the expense of the ability to enjoy life. You will continue

to experience anxiety or fear at the idea that the secret may somehow come out in a way that you are not prepared to deal with."

"Scott, you are my angel! How do you know exactly what to say to me, it is like God sent you to me," Maya said to Scott lovingly.
"Well, thank god I'm an atheist," Scott joked. He always made Maya laugh at that joke.

"Well, I better start from the beginning," Maya chuckled.

We had a very comfortable life. Mom and dad made sure we went to the best schools and always provided the best they could for their daughters. If only they knew Khalil would bring such pain and suffering for years to come.

"Did you know we had another sister?" Not waiting for Scott to answer, Maya continued.

My parents had lost a child to gastroenteritis. Her name was Renuka she was merely 18 months old, and the entire family contracted GT. I don't think that mom and dad ever got over the loss of their child. They still feel tied to her. It does not matter how long ago it happened, to this day, the love they feel for her is so powerful. That is the love of a parent.

Her death caused dad to become a more stable father. He had stopped going out every weekend with his friends. Mom always said that Renuka's death made Bali a better father. When I was born two years later, Bali doted on me, and I guess I became his favorite daughter to this day. But as I got older, he left the affection giving to mom and concentrated on our hobbies and education.

After Rania left, Daya and I shared the back room. I felt like a big girl. You know that to this day we are still close, but we are getting ahead of the story. It is so sad that Khalil's abuse went on for far too long and affected me in unmentionable ways. Today as I look back on the saga that dominated my dad's decision to marry his daughters to people that

The Contriving

he barely knew or didn't know, at all, I think of the irony of how it all worked out or didn't work out, I should say.

My dad's father, his name was Suma, had built an empire of investment properties in Kitty and was a very respectful man. I don't remember him, but there are so many stories I've heard about him. Rania was only nineteen. She had recently graduated and had topped the country in her GCE exams. It was then she was supposed to get married when she was abducted by her fiancé.

"What?" Scott exclaimed in astonishment. "Kidnapped by her fiancé? "What the heck!"
Maya had said it so matter-of-factly.

To be honest, I still don't know what exactly happened, so what I am telling is what I saw, and what I presumed happened.

Veer was introduced to the family by a priest who was also my mom's maternal uncle Raja in Berbice. Veer and his family just finished a three-day Ramayana Yagna, sponsored by Veer. Veer came a long way just to do this ritual and he impressed Uncle Raja immediately. I clearly remember when we met Veer. It was in August 1980, a Friday morning, during the summer school break. It was a nice sunny morning. I was in the garden, in a hammock doing my favorite thing, reading Nancy Drew's *Mystery of the 99 Steps*. I remember squinting as the sun was coming through the leaves when I heard a car pull up on the sidewalk. It was my mom's uncle Raja. I had always loved Uncle Raja and was happy to see him.

I remember putting down my book in the hammock and sliding on my rubber flip-flops.
You know me, I never like walking with bare feet. I remember hugging him and he smiled and hugged me and asked for my mom. I told him she was inside. He followed me in with his entire entourage. I noticed this young handsome man beside him, and he smiled at me too. Uncle Raja showed his entourage the lovely flower garden that my dad was

so proud of. He was an avid gardener and loved to spend his spare time tending to his rose plants, Hibiscus, Croton etc.

All of our gardens are beautiful. I think I take after my dad for that green thumb. I hurried into the house to get my mom and dad and tell them that their guests had arrived. Daya, Nadia, and I, stayed in the back of the house by the kitchen.

Alloo balls and Phoulourie, which were prepared ahead of time in anticipation of the guests, were set out on the coffee table.

Rania had to serve the 'soft drinks.' This was the chance for Veer to be introduced to Rania. Us girls were peering through the glass openings of the kitchen cupboards that had a view straight to the living room.

I remember giggling and teasing Rania every time she came back to the kitchen. But she seemed to take a quick liking to Veer, and who can blame her? Veer was extremely good-looking and charismatic. He could have easily been a male model and he was adored by the fair sex for his good looks. And he knew it. He played it well.

He had a casual hairstyle, jumbled sometimes but mostly neat and flowing. He has crescent-of-moon eyebrows that were thin and narrow. He carried his imperious nose well. He had angular cheekbones carved down towards a flinty jaw with a chiseled chin. He had a manly physique and glided with an athletic grace, without skipping a beat. His brown eyes were round and gleamed with the vigor of youth. His cologne, which, had a hint of honey, tobacco and wood, had the women folks swooning in his presence. They would a make very good-looking couple.

I always thought Rania was so beautiful, with midnight black hair that flowed softly around her shoulders. She had a demure and personality that was very ladylike, unlike me."

Maya laughed.
"You are, though,' Scott said.

The Contriving

I wasn't back then. I was more of an adventurous child and Rania was blatantly condescending toward my pompous bright and cheerful personality. Rania was more reserved, calm, and collected, sometimes even shy. Socializing was a little tricky for her, so she did not have many friends, nor did she have close friendships with people in school.

Growing up as the younger sister, I saw her as never dramatic, and often very capable in terms of managing her emotions. She was self-sufficient and enjoyed her alone time.

I remember how I used to like to read in her bedroom because it was in the back room which made it bright, sunny, and breezy. I eventually shared that room with Daya when Rania left.

Rania would often drag me from her room so that she and Daya could be alone. I used to pretend I was older and wanted to hang out with the older sisters. They used to tease me and call me "force ripe" and "quarter bottle."

Rania was more of an introvert, and she was comfortable with herself and can spend hours and hours thinking about things without realizing where the time has gone.

Limelight is not something that she, nor Daya sought out – at all! Unlike Nadia and I. We had many friends and were more of the social types. And Tania was too young at the time.

It is not that Rania and Daya do not want to be acknowledged or appreciated, just that they would rather not have a lot of attention directed at them. Both Rania and Daya preferred to stay in the shadows. They do not often dress to stand out – they did not want the added attention this might bring. They are more conservative in their choice of clothes, hairstyle, and makeup, and tend to choose comfort primarily. Their overall appearance mirrors their underlying nature.

Rania wore cosmopolitan clothes and had a very shapely figure. She had a glossy chestnut complexion. She wore her eyebrows in a slender arch which she kept shapely once a week. Her eyelashes were thick, dense, and full of volume, with hazel-colored eyes which amplified her glamorous beauty.

She was five feet three inches tall, average among Indian girls. She got attractive marriage proposals being the eldest of Bali and Premika's five girls, but she rejected every one of them until she met Veer.

Marriage is supposed to be between two people who love each other, but what happens when it is an arranged marriage? This thought probably never crossed your mind, and to be honest, it never crossed mine either. Although, the interesting part about all this is, that my parents are living proof of an arranged marriage. It is not a simple task to fall in love with a stranger, but my parents proved to me that it could work out, even though it is a long road to success.

How it works is first, the groom gets some background information about the bride. A general description of how she looks, what things she can do like cooking/cleaning, and the level of education she has. The parents of the bride will let the parents of the groom know all the details about her through the priest, and that is the only way he finds out about the bride. Usually, if the groom likes what he has heard then his family will meet with the bride's family. During this time everyone will gather at the bride's house and have refreshments. This is the first time they will see each other. If everything goes well and both the groom and the bride mutually like each other, then they move on to the next step. My parents have the funniest stories about when they first met. Mom spilled drinks all over my dad. And when they finally talked and shared birthdays, mom thought that dad was teasing her and that he had already known her birthday, which was the same as his.

Bizarre Occurrence
The next phase in Rania's story is the unlikely confluence that sets the stage for a bizarre and intense story of love, betrayal, deceit, and secrets.

Since both Veer and Rania readily agreed to the arranged marriage, both families met again to plan the engagement, picking the date, time,

The Contriving

location, and how much dowry. Then as plans were being made for the wedding, Veer made a bizarre request, which to this day I cannot fathom why my parents agreed to it.

He had already returned to Canada while his older sister and my parents were making all the arrangements for the wedding. Out of nowhere, he demanded that Rania visit Canada for two weeks. At first, my parents were puzzled by this unusual request and wanted to know the reason for this strange demand. Veer said he wanted to ensure that Rania would like it in Canada. I remember thinking, what a bizarre request. But what was even stranger to me was that eventually, my parents agreed to this. I did not understand why they would agree to it, as this was very unusual in our tradition. You would have to be married to be able to travel and live with a man, regardless of if it was only for two weeks.

But it happened. It was agreed that Tania would accompany Rania to Canada.

Although still quite young, she was the only one who was able to be the chaperone at the time. Daya was working and could not take time off on such short notice, and both Nadia and I were in the middle of finals for high school. To be honest, I was so taken up with exams, I barely knew what was going on around me at the time, but I do remember their sudden vacation was quite hush-hush and under wraps. I don't believe even my grandparents were aware of these arrangements. I don't recall the exact day they left, but I do remember that mom was calling Canada every other day to find out how they were doing.

It was a big secret from the other family members. It was not like two people keeping a secret from one or many other family members. We were all so close to each other. Our cousins, aunts, and uncles were next door. How would they not know that Rania had gone away for two weeks? What would we say to our cousins who came to play with Tania? The only person outside of our home who knew was my mom's sister, Lana. And her nickname was "secret agent, as she was so good at keeping secrets."

We were not allowed to talk about it and honestly, at the time I did not know who knew and who did not. This internal secret, known by some and not others, created sub-groupings, drawing lines between those who knew and those left unaware. In some cases, that line may be appropriate. I remember feeling loyalty to my father and mother, but it also made me feel like I may slip up and betray them by telling my other cousins or even my friends at school.

Scott smiled and interjected, 'This position is called a split loyalty, and it can eat away at a secret holder caught between somebody in the know and somebody left unaware. For children, this position is particularly corrosive as it involves one's parents."

Maya agreed.

Shared family secrets are pieces of information known within the family but forbidden to outsiders. Some of these pieces of information actually increase closeness and cohesion by creating an internal culture that feels special. That said, shared family secrets are also more likely to center on taboo topics, such as abuse within the family. People cite many reasons for maintaining family secrets, including protecting the family from judgment, dealing with possible consequences, and privacy.

These secrets create a boundary between the family and the outside world and may pressure individual family members to limit their outside relationships to protect against the secret getting out. Family members may feel trapped by the secret and struggle to create close ties outside the family. These types of secrets may also lead families to internalize shame.

Our family was a very private one. Yet, as I look back, I can't help but think that on several occasions, the lines between privacy and secrecy became very blurred. I am sure that this is different in every family.

Birthday celebrations and family traditions, like soirees and musical evenings, did keep our families together cohesively and lovingly, especially on my dad's side of the family.

The Contriving

I knew that these secrets were very taboo subjects and, once revealed, would create strife.

It is sad that the act of keeping individual secrets can lead to further isolation and anxiety, simply about the secret emerging. I always felt that these family secrets created a sense of loyalty, based not on a sense of connection, but instead on feelings of fear and shame should the secret come out.

I wish I could tell my family that they need to examine themselves and the way information moves through them. Only then can they come together and start to assess and address these family secrets and the role each member has in keeping them, if any.

Anyway, as the week went by, mom's calls were more frequent. Mom always seemed uneasy after the calls.

There seems to be some awkwardness as it appeared that Veer's real living situation was not what he claimed to be, but even then, mom was not saying much to us. Something mystifying was happening – but as I said, I was too caught up in final exams to even worry about it at the time. It was the last week of our exams and Nadia and I fell into a routine of going to bed early and waking up in the wee hours of the morning to study when it was quiet and there was no hustle and bustle from the outside world. We did miss out on some of the family discussions.

The Friday after our last exams, mom and dad agreed to take us to the Liberty Cinema to see the latest Bollywood movie "Dard." It was our reward for all the hard work we put in studying for months.

What happened when we arrived home from the movies was the most baffling and unfathomable circumstance that I still cannot understand.

"What happened?" Scott asked, even more puzzled.

Maya paused and took a bite out of the cookies Scott had placed on the coffee table and sipped at her coffee. Scott makes the most delicious coffee. She tried to find words to explain what happened, but the words did not come, as she still never understood what had transpired that day. Permyak and Bali ensured that nothing was discussed in front of the girls.

"So, what happened," Scott urged, noticing that Maya seemed lost in thoughts.

Well, it was just so bizarre. Rania and Tania were waiting for us at my Aunt Glenda's house. Aunt Glenda and Uncle Kris lived behind us.

"What the heck?" Scott exclaimed. "Why did you guys go to the cinema on the same day they were coming home?"
"No, that was the bizarre thing, we didn't know they were coming home," Maya explained. They came home almost a week before their vacation ended."
"Why?" Scott was beyond puzzled. Maya shook her head. "I don't know, to this day no one speaks about it, and at the time, it seemed to be a top secret and the explanation to us girls was that they wanted to surprise us. Looking back now, that was all bull shit."

Maya's recollection of this situation was vague, but she remembered that Rania seemed befuddled, but Tania appeared even more puzzled and disoriented as if she did not even know she was coming home. The whole situation seemed to stump Premika and Bali, and they seem so embarrassed about the whole thing.

I remembered that mom and dad looked both shocked and uncomfortable when Aunty Glenda came running through the back gates to tell us that Rania and Tania were at her house. They were at a complete loss for words, and quietly took Rania and Tania home through the dark back stairs, with the rest of us girls, walking quietly behind them, all too bewildered and baffled to say anything. We were ushered to bed, as mom and dad talked to Rania in whispers. Life went on and wedding plans were back in full swing.

The Contriving

Maya paused. The memories were emerging along with the emotions that left her numb and dazed. She couldn't continue anymore. That evening, Scott and Maya went out for dinner. Scott thought it was a good idea to take Maya back to the Greek restaurant where they had their first date. They had the exact thing they had ordered on their first date. Maya had chicken souvlaki and a salad and Scott had Gyro, potatoes, and a salad. As they sipped the Pink Zinfandel, they reflected on the first date and how they spent hours right here at the restaurant. It was a happy evening, and since Greek food was another one Scott's favorites, they even dropped off a chicken souvlaki dinner plate for him.

Chapter Five

Vanishing Act

The next day Maya decided it was her turn to make breakfast, and she was eager to continue her story. She wanted to tell Scott everything, she was feeling so much better already, just talking and letting go of the pent-up emotions, the secrets that she had kept for so long.

She made "bake and salt fish" for breakfast, while Scott did some laundry.

Sitting in the sunny room after breakfast, Maya didn't expect to feel sad and emotional. She was also feeling guilty, for sharing all the family's long-kept secrets. She knew she shouldn't be feeling guilty and wanted to share this with Scott. She knew she wanted to share everything with Scott, even the darkness of these long-forgotten details. Maya levered herself up from the sofa, left the comfort of the beautiful sunroom, with a sense of traversing a portal, and found Scott in the kitchen, stirring pasta sauce. She watched him for a moment before he sensed her. He seemed preoccupied with something, the wooden spoon doing a little more than troubling the surface of the food.

When he sensed her, he turned and half smiled, evidently trying to assess Maya's state of mind, which ironically, she was doing the same. He walked over and hugged her from behind.

Maya loves his bear hugs. He squeezed her and she felt a rush of adrenaline through her body.
As she turned to him, she saw the question in his eyes.
"Yes, I am okay," she reassured him. "Are you?' she asked.
"Yes, I am just worried about you, resurfacing all these horrible memories is not easy," Scott said gently.
"I am thinking of you, and how all of what I am sharing must be very daunting for you," Maya replied.
Scott flipped the dishcloth he was holding and cleared his throat. "I am fine babe, it is a lot to take in, but I am here for you that is what matters." He was wearing the apron his sister had sent for his birthday with the slogan "Kiss the chef." It was the same apron he had worn the first time he made her dinner.
He did look good, sleek, and composed as always. Maya thought of that first dinner at his house, and how nervous she was.
She smiled as she remembered how she thought his apron was funny at the time.

As Scott left the Ragu to simmer, they took a bottle of chilled Rose wine and their glasses out to the sunroom and settled back into the sofa. It was mid-afternoon, but as Scott's famous words were 'it is the double-digit on the clock' meaning they could drink any time of day. Maya always thought it was a German thing.

After they had settled in, Maya continued.

The wedding day came fast. Finally, a wedding in the Maraj family, after so many years. For my dad, his first daughter was getting married. Maybe he was thinking, 'one down, and four to go.'

Maya and Scott chuckled.

Veer had arrived from Canada a few days before the wedding and was staying with his sister in Mahaica Creek. He had borrowed my dad's sports car to get around, as everyone was too busy preparing for the wedding and had no time to drive him back and forth. Veer loved that car the moment he laid eyes on it. This was the same car I crashed into the garbage can when Assam was trying to teach me to drive a few months later.

Maya smiled and Scott shook his head, to this day she won't get behind a stick shift car.

The morning of the matticore night, I remember waking up before the sun was up and the chickens clucking in the yard. Everything was set. The word extravagant rarely does Indian weddings justice. They are fabulous, outrageous, and utterly extravagant, like Sandy's wedding on Long Island.

They are week-long productions of epic proportions, the sheer drama, costume, music, and sumptuous food leaves the guests stunned – but in a magical way! Rania's wedding was not any different, and the big day was supposed to be remembered as a social triumph for the Maraj family.

Rania had chosen a classically elegant off-white wedding dress for the reception, a full-length red and gold lengha with a bejewelled dupatta. I didn't pay much attention to the wedding outfits. I can't even remember what I was going to wear for the wedding. Amid all the hustle and bustle of getting prepared, Veer came walking into the yard. I remembered thinking, what the heck is he doing here? It is unusual for the bridegroom to be at the bride's house on the matticore day. He should be having his own matticore preparations, but he claimed to want to take Rania jewelry shopping instead.

Mom was reluctant to send Rania. It was matticore day after all. After much smooth-talking and persuading from Veer, she finally agreed. I don't think my dad even knew that Rania had left with Veer. He would not have allowed it. But mom was more lenient, and Veer was persuasive. Oh, was he ever a sweet talker? No one was available to chaperone Rania as everyone had chores that needed to be completed before the weekend-long event. And I was busy doing what I did best. I was preparing and rehearsing the Bollywood dances.

Dad had his eight-piece band all getting ready that day. They were testing the sound system, as the uncles prepared the food for matticore night. The band was dad's hobby.

Indian singing and dancing were the evening's entertainment. Music, dancing, and showing off! The preparation throughout the day had gone smoothly for the matticore night. Guests were starting to slowly trickle in, as Assam entertained everyone, like *Shah Rukh Khan, in Dil Wale Dulhan Liye Jayege, dancing* and joking around with everyone. All the ladies in the family loved him and favored him. Little did they know he was ensuring that they loved him before he made his move on the big proposal. We will get back to this. Let me continue with the wedding.

Scott smiled. He can see Assam being the life of the party. He still is.

The wedding was well planned. It was just like the image of growing up watching Bollywood movies, with all the extravagance and lavishness of the typical Indian wedding. This was no different, it was going to be bigger and fatter than the big fat Greek wedding. And traditional like *Dil Wale Dulhan Liye Jayege.*

Maya and Scott watched that movie only last week, and the traditions and cultures, the hustle and bustle of the wedding, and planning reminded her of the Indian weddings back home. Indians are known for their love for elaborate weddings, and Guyana, a country with diverse cultures calls for diverse wedding customs and traditions. Each family was unique in its way, and so are the wedding rituals and beliefs that come along with it.

The Maraj family's big fat Indian weddings usually begin with the bride's parents offering gifts and sweets to the groom's family in return for gifts

Vanishing Act

for the bride, the parents and the sisters and sweets, like mitha, peera etc., from the groom's family before the matticore night.

"What about the Mehendi and Sangeet ceremony?" Scott asked, remembering this special ceremony from Sandy's wedding they had attended in New York only a month ago. Maya was pleasantly surprised that he remembered the names of these ceremonies which are filled with dancing, drama, and music.

The bride and everyone attending the wedding traditionally apply beautiful designs of henna on their hands at the Mehendi ceremony. On the day of the wedding, the bride is adorneda with chooda, a set of red and gold bangles that are purified in a liquid mixture containing milk and rose petals.

Chooda is an important part of a Hindu ceremony. Although it is a Punjabi tradition, our family still does this. It is said that our paternal great grandfather, was of Punjabi descent. My dad says he remembers him in his turbans riding horses to round up the cows. So, some of our family traditions are a combination of Punjabi and Uttar Pradesh customs.

This particular one is one of the most evident marks of a new bride. Not only that, but it is also known to bring good luck to newlyweds. Red is a very important color for a married woman, as it is believed to strengthen the bond between a couple.

On the matticore night, also called the "cook night," the ceremony begins with prayers to Mother Earth, where the mother of the bride or groom performs this special puja. The female guests must arrive on time to go along with the mother, following the 'Tassa' crew, to an especially scouted-out clean area where the puja is performed. After the puja, the procession heads back to the wedding house for the matticore procedures.

The pandit will conduct this ceremony, which is then follows the Haldi ceremony or, as Guyanese call it 'rubbing dye." This is a paste of sandalwood, turmeric, rosewater, and mustard oil that is said to give the bride a radiant, beautiful glow. Once the Haldi ceremony is done, the bride starts getting ready for the wedding. Our family followed the traditional rituals of an Indian wedding, which is a grand occasion, very colourful and very lavish, with an enormous amount of pomp and show. The festivities usually begin at least a week in advance. The guests, the get-togethers, the music, and the dance all are a part of this extravaganza.

It is no silent affair. It is one of the most crucial events in the life of every Indian mother, father, daughter, son, brother or sister, the word 'Indian Wedding' carries the whole baggage of an entire fortune which people did not mind spending. An Indian wedding is not just a day's affair. It's a celebration before marriage.

I was the ambiguous child, the entertainer, always making everyone laugh. I used to do the 'hellfire' dance for fun but didn't want my dad to see me, so whenever he entered the room as I was dancing, I would freeze, scared that he would get mad at the wild dancing.

Scott laughed, knowing how fun Maya is when it comes to such things.

I was imaginative and creative. When I came home from watching any movie, I would pretend I was a Bollywood movie star. In Bollywood movies, women bow and touch their man's feet, and also the priest's feet. Although, I was never comfortable with that and thought I would never do that. To this day, I refused to touch the pandit's feet, as most Hindus do. I do not feel comfortable doing that at all.

Unfortunately, Bollywood movies also taught us that women were supposed to be submissive. The elders live their lives like that still, and watching my family and sisters, I saw how the women did the same thing.

Back then, watching Indian movies I used to cry a lot for the heroine, not knowing that my faith would be similar.

Vanishing Act

Like a dramatic Bollywood movie, when I married Jason not knowing him, not seeing what he looks like, not falling in love. I thought that getting married would allow me to leave my dark deep secret behind but that was just not the case.

Anyway, back to the story.

Guests were starting to arrive, just as mom realized that Rania had not returned yet. It was about the same time that Veer walked through the front gates, asking for her. I was in the front, getting ready to go upstairs when he walked in. I was puzzled that she was not with him. He proceeded to talk to my mom, saying that he went to the bathroom in the restaurant. When he came back, she was gone! He thought she left and come home, as it was getting late.

I remembered my heart sank as my mom let out a sharp scream and clutched her heart. I ran to get my dad as Veer and mom got into a heated argument. Mom demanded to know why he would leave her alone. Initially, our first conclusion was that she was taken by the military because they had attacked and raided the home so many times before. They knew that we were having this big wedding and we immediately were afraid that something bad had happened to her.

Mom came into the middle of the room, and Veer followed, still trying to explain what happened, but mom didn't seem to be listening. She shook her head, profusely, as if wanting not to believe what was happening.

Dad was pacing the room, as I called mom's uncle, who was the chief of police.

Mom shut her eyes, then opened them again, to look at the picture of Rania on the mantle. Then she placed her hands on her chest. She whispered in a shortly ragged breath, that she can't breathe, she struggled to pull in a full breath. Dad put her to sit down.

I remembered that as soon as Veer said he did not have Rania, my uncles were suspicious. Then, they grabbed him by the shirt and brought him upstairs. They were suspicious of him now, but I would say I was suspicious of him from the beginning, and even more so after Rania returned from Canada with no explanation as to what happened. These things were not sitting right with me at all, even though I was a young girl, it was just not right. But then, I had an imaginative mind, I was always being told that I read too many Nancy Drew mysteries.

My uncles dragged him up the stairs and sat him down in the living room. They did not give him a chance to speak but indicated that we had called the police.

Veer glared at me as the police lights flash through the windows.

"Why did you have to call the police?" He questioned me, just as Chief of Police Roman came up the stairs. He did not know much, as I didn't want to give many details on the phone, with Veer right there, but I am sure Chief Roman heard the panic in my voice. Besides, he always felt obligated to my mom for taking care of his children when he was younger and worked long hours. Chief Roman started asking Veer a series of questions, but his story did not seem to add up.

That night, Veer was arrested for kidnapping. When he showed up at our home that evening, I am positive that he didn't expect that he would be the one to get questioned and arrested. He was in a rage but with little reason. He was ranting and raving, claiming he was being disadvantaged and treated as a criminal because our mom's uncle was the chief of police.

It was the most embarrassing and humiliating situation, when they took the bridegroom away in front of all the guests, even though he was not handcuffed, they took him in a cruiser.

With my overactive, Nancy Drew detective's brain, I had to know what was happening, so Uncle Randy and I decided to follow. When we got to the police station, they had already read him his Miranda rights, and he was handcuffed to a chair with his arms behind his back. We spoke with Chief Roman. He stated that Veer was maintaining his innocence, insisting that he did not know what happened to Rania and we must be hiding her from him. What an absurd remark, I thought that was.

One of the police officers took off the handcuffs and Veer rubbed his wrists as he glared at me.

Maya paused. Her recollection of that evening was somewhat vague. Years later, even Bali and Premika claimed that their recollection was also vague, on the details of that evening. It was as if they all wanted to shut out this painful, humiliating, and devastating event of that evening and the days that followed.

Even years later, Chief Roman seemed to have the clearest memory of how Rania allegedly went missing.
He related to mom that Veer was not telling the truth. He knew that Veer seemed dishonest, from the moment he met Veer. His words to mom and dad were "I am genuinely concerned some harm has come to her." Veer denied that he did any such thing.

That evening and late into the night, Chief Ramon's investigating officers questioned witnesses who were outside the bank, and most of them confirmed that an argument ensued between Rania and Veer, and Veer seem to be in a jealous rage.

Later both veer and Rania unequivocally denied all allegations of any argument in this regard.
Veer's words were "This was a private issue ... and in no way resulted from a jealous rage."

But eyewitness accounts contradicted this.

Chief Ramon was very concerned that there was an incident of disruptive behavior that occurred. What appeared to be a disagreement between the two may have turned violent, leading to Rania's disappearance.

Witnesses said Veer appeared very jealous and paranoid.

Veer was furious when he saw me and Uncle Randy at the police station. He screamed at me in a threatening tone, 'Is this how you want it to go? Your family needs to stop lying. Wait until I get out, I will deal with you.'

I went up to him and said, 'Veer calm down, you need to relax.' He turned to me, violently, and told me not to involve myself. I backed off to go through the side door, to where he could not see me and Uncle Randy, but he became more aggressive, knocking on the glass, threatening me, and pointing. He kept shouting, 'I know what you're trying to do.'

Uncle Randy and I went through the door, and they placed handcuffs on him again.
Chief Ramon said that he placed a call to Veer's family friend and told them that Veer had been arrested for kidnapping. As I walked away, with my emphatic nature, I thought to myself, that Veer actually sounded really scared, and I felt sorry for him.
His family showed up along with his 80-year-old dad, who was rambling about Veer committing bigamy. He sounded really scared too and my heart went out to him. Nobody was paying much attention to this old man. It was too bad, although he was always talking nonstop, and did not always make sense, he was telling the truth, as we will find out later.

Chief Ramon and his team continued their search and investigation for the next few hours, trying to track down Rania. After talking to witnesses at the bank, they headed to Arapaima restaurant, where Veer said they had lunch. Indeed, they went to the restaurant. Witnesses did state that Veer went to the restroom, and they recalled him saying that Rania was gone upon his return. He asked around but, no one had noticed her leaving. Some witnesses even claimed that they thought they saw her going to the restroom as well. Everyone was now looking for her. One witness said he saw her outside the bank, next to the restaurant. It is believed that she might have gotten into someone's van. Nothing was adding up and details became more tangled as the night went on.

The search continued all that night. I will never forget that night. It was such a traumatic night. No one slept. My uncles had already sent home the guests before I came back from the police station. We had so much food leftover that we had to take all of it to the nearby orphanage.

There I met a cute little 'Dougal" boy for the first time. He must have been about 5 years old. It was a start of a beautiful relationship that lasted until I left Guyana. I used to visit him every other day. I am sorry, to diverge once again - back to the story.

Maya smiled at Scott.

Police Chief Ramon came the next morning and told my parents that the detectives are "no more along" than they were last night, on the case.

Hours after her disappearance, the police were still interrogating Veer for information but were at a loss for what could have happened.

Someone disappearing is suspicious, but there are no signs of foul play, nothing out of the ordinary at Veer's family house either. His sister's house was found empty, with the lights and air conditioning on, the back door unlocked, and her dog in the house, with no food or water. She too had come to the police station with their dad, and she had immediately claimed that she said she was at the family house for days, preparing for the wedding, and did not see Rania.

At the time all of this was happening, we were living in the moment, not realizing how unfavorable the whole situation was. Veer insisted he could prove his innocence and was quite adamant that he had nothing to do with Rania's disappearance.

But I had a weird feeling in my stomach. I knew something was wrong. The police tried her friend's house but, she didn't have a lot of friends, she hung out with Daya and our cousins that was it.

When asked what he thinks happened, Veer said he thought someone in the neighborhood is either responsible or, at the very least, saw something. He still insisted that someone is hiding her.

The Ungracious Daughter

Chief Ramon said that he had run through every scenario in his brain, but nothing added up. My parents went back to the city to help with the search again. I stayed behind and Daya and I were given the difficult task of sending the guests home. We didn't know what to tell them, then Daya came up with the brilliant idea of saying that Veer's mother had died, and we had to cancel the wedding. Everyone was so sympathetic that we felt terribly guilty. But as we started cleaning up, taking down decorations, and sending back all the rental chairs, the feeling of guilt went away. By this time mom and dad returned with no further information than before.

As we continued to clean up, to our astonishment, Rania suddenly appeared in the yard, disoriented, and confused as if she had been drugged. We quickly took her upstairs. After gulping down 2 glasses of water, she told her story. And boy! What a story!

Rania related that Veer did take her to the jewelry store. After they were done shopping, they went for lunch at Arapaima restaurant. She drank iced tea and remembered it was very cold, and she had a "brain freeze." Then they went to the bank.

Rania said that she was standing outside the bank, waiting for Veer, when someone pushed her to the ground. She said she screamed and fell to her side but before she could get up, she heard a car coming and someone shouting, "Open the door!"

When she realized that someone was attacking her, she started screaming louder, for help, but no one was around as the city was shutting down for the evening.

She attempted to free herself, but the kidnapper shoved her into a "maxi taxi" and closed the door. She said she struggled to free herself because the kidnappers were so strong. She couldn't remember anything else after that, because they put a cloth with liquid over her mouth, she thinks maybe it was Chloroform, which is used by criminals to knock out, daze, or even murder victims. It was not long before she passed out.

Vanishing Act

She said when she woke up later, with the worst headache of her life, she was laying on a bed in a small old dusty pink room. She was confused and dazed for a bit, but then she remembered what had happened at the bank.

She headed to the door and started knocking it hard. She said she was screaming at the top of her lungs "get me out of here, get me out of here."

Someone responded, "Hey you, we are coming in a second."

She stopped yelling and put her head against the door trying to hear something. She said that it was then she heard Veer's voice. She was shocked and baffled. She heard their footsteps coming towards her and she was terrified. She took some steps back and the door opened. She was surprised to see Veer standing there with a young man. She said that she was now more confused than ever, then she was angry and demanded to know whom the hell brought her there.

Veer explained that it was he who had her kidnapped. It was a plan, and he had an explanation for it. Rania screamed at him, calling him an idiot, and that he almost gave her a heart attack. She told him that she was going to call the police. He got scared and she saw that he started sweating.

She looked at him and he was visibly shaken. She felt sorry for saying that. She told Veer that she thought it was a bad gang or the military that kidnapped her to blackmail her dad.

Veer explained why he brought her here. And what an explanation it was!

"That is uncanny," Scott said, interested to hear the rest of this bizarre story.

Maya shook her head in agreement .

She took a deep breath. "I need a drink to continue, as you won't believe his explanation," she said.

Scott couldn't wait to hear the rest. He went to the kitchen to check on the Ragu, which they were having for dinner.
He made them another set of drinks and grabbed some salsa and Tostitos chips. Maya makes the best homemade Salsa.

As they settled back in, Scott turned off the TV. The dim lights came in from the moonlit garden that was off the sunroom. It lit up Maya's face, making her glow in the darkened room. She looked so beautiful, Scott paused, not wanting to disrupt that picture, but then she looked up and beckoned him to come back on the couch.

So apparently Veer was married! Remember I said that no one was paying attention to the old man?

Well, he was the only one speaking the truth.

Veer pleaded with Rania. He was married in America to a Trinidadian woman who was refusing to give him a divorce. If he goes through with marrying Rania, he would be committing bigamy. Veer knew that the odds were against him. He probably told Rania less, because of his narcissistic temperament, and because it was probably simply becoming too difficult, to tell the truth.

Rania told of how she realized she was missing her own wedding and begged Veer to bring her back. Veer tried to explain that there can't be a wedding, but Rania was too worried to realize what he was saying. Besides, Veer continued, they were stuck in "the creek" with no one to bring them over to the mainland. They had to wait it out tonight until the fisherman came back the next day. Mahaica creek is a village located in Demerara. Most of the houses in this area are on their own, tiny little islands. The only way of getting around is by small canoes, of which each house had one. The fisherman must have used this one to get back to the mainland.

Maya ended her story there that evening, explaining to Scott that she realized that some of the stories may be foggy or confusing to him, but it is how she remembered them.

They had invited the kids over for dinner, but Kyle and Melena already had plans. Sean and Ryder arrived just as the pasta was ready. After a wonderful evening of light conversation and delicious food, Ryder and Sean bid farewell. As they were at the door, Ryder hugged Maya. "I am so happy for you mom, you found your person," and then she turned to give Scott a long hug, catching him off guard. He was not used to all the affection.

Chapter Six

Arresting Development

*T*he next day, Maya continued the story while they cooked in the kitchen. They were invited to a BBQ at Daya and Assam's that evening, and Maya had promised to make her famous potato salad.

It was not a straightforward joy at the reunion. It was deflated. Although they must have been relieved at finding their daughter, I am sure that mom and dad had many questions about unknowns that they did not even want to delve into. It was all about showing face and keeping everything hush-hush, not letting anyone find out what really happened or that their potential son-in-law could be a kidnapper and bigamist.

I always wondered why they brushed it under the carpet, and never really talked about it again. But I remember clearly when Rania came home, I saw the frustrations in their eyes and their behaviors as they tried to understand what happened. I had a feeling that she may have threatened to disappear again. They felt betrayed.

For my part, I felt as though Rania was a stranger in the house, and I was so unsure of how to deal with all the stress, distrust, and doubts. But mom and dad seemed too scared to talk about it, and for fear that she may disappear again. And I was not sure whether it was okay to talk about it. About what happened, I had so many unanswered questions for Rania, but I was afraid to open Pandora's Box. I was so confused and frustrated because Rania's story was just not adding up. And you know me, I need it to be clear like black and white and it was muddy, dark, and gray.

It was nearly three days now. Rania seemed like a small, frightened child and spoke in whispers, which wasn't like her at all.

I remembered sitting for nearly three hours, in the rain in our backyard, hoping to get some clarity on this. I could not understand how my parents were not talking about it.

My mom did not seem to know what to say to Rania, so she decided to write her a letter. I think it was hard for her to face the facts. I remember the contents of that letter clearly.

Dear Rania,

When you were a baby, you were like a little elf. The entire family was so filled with joy at your pixie-like presence, full of curiosity, wonder, and joy. I remember the glorious hours I spent nursing you, rocking you, and singing lullabies to you, while you smiled up at me. When I would stop singing, you would ask for more. When you were four years old, you walked into the kitchen one day, and without any lead-in, asked "Mummy, when am I going to get my harmonium?" I laughed at the seemingly impromptu nature of this question. We had never talked about this before, although you had heard a lot of classical music coming from your dad's practice sessions.
When we did get you a harmonium at age six, your teacher said he was sure you had played the harmonium in a former life. You were

a natural. I guess that is why you asked such seemingly random questions. You were too young to remember. Your teacher told me one day, without an ounce of irony, "This child has been here before. She is an old soul." You were so smart that you moved ahead two grades. But did it hurt you in other ways? I can only surmise. Your intellect was not restricted to academics, however. You were a keen observer of the human condition. You were a gift to our family — a family that is now suffering so much pain — and we need you.

You seem like a stranger now. But as happens sometimes in families, the dynamics become set and each person has a role to play. I am heartbroken that yours was to be this person that we cannot seem to understand or know. I want to rip up the pages of the past and rewrite them. The only way I can do that is to tell you how sorry I am.

I see how hard you were trying to not let us in, and my heart breaks. I love you and I am so sad about this whole situation. You are precious beyond words, and I love you so fiercely. When you were in your early teens, you fell in love with the idea of being a teacher — teaching kindergarten children. I remember when you played Mother Mary in the school play, putting the entire assembly of parents in tears. It was just like you, to tug at heartstrings, to display your love of people in a way that made everyone want to be you when they grow up. I was so proud of you.

One of my favorite memories of you is when you would go out into the pasture with your latest Hardy Boys book and swing up onto the back of your grandfather's horse, lying there while he grazed, the two of you as comfortable with each other as if you sprang from the same root. That memory is so imprinted on my soul that it will go with me to my dying day.

I'm scared to talk to you now. Or anyone for that matter. I'm scared for a few reasons, but mostly I'm scared of receiving judgment or of bringing judgment upon my child. Being the only mother or wife in the Maraj family that works, we already encounter some judgments, so do I want this additional label attached to our family? Do I want other families to avoid us and label us as "too much drama" for having had this happen to us? Because there is so much that isn't said about kidnapping or whatever it may be called. So much that I didn't know until after you were gone. As an extension of the previous point, allowing Veer to take you shopping on the matticore day, is my fault. I should not have allowed it. I did not want to call the police, but we had no choice.

For, I didn't want my daughter to experience police intervention. I also know how much you loved Veer; it would have traumatized you to watch him get arrested or to experience being taken away in a police car away from our house. I pray that we can get past this.

You're loving Mom

Rania read the letter and left it on the dressing room table. That is how I got a hold of it and read it. She seemed not to be aware of the effects what had happened, nor did she seem happy to see us when she returned. She didn't show any emotions towards the letter. I presumed that she was also conflicted because we had never been apart for that length of time before, and she resented our intrusion or questions about what happened.

Me, I was overjoyed to have her home, but I also knew that she was not the same. It felt like we lost our big sister, even though she was back at home. There would always be a part of me that had lost her. That week of her life will always be etched on my heart, and I don't know that I will ever feel completely whole again as a younger sister, losing the spirit of that big sister I looked up to, not only academically, but in every aspect of being my big sister.

Coming home was the end of the worst, but the beginning of what was far more to come.

Sadly, the ordeal wasn't over once Rania was home. She was jumpy and seemed to be experiencing a bit of depression.

For the first time in my life, I saw my dad was disorganized, out of place, and not going to work for days. I wondered if he felt inadequate and unworthy of being our dad.

He seemed so stressed out and anxious about the incident that he did overreact at a few of Rania's outbursts, likely caused by her stress from the incident. For the most part, people outside of our family didn't know exactly what happened. It was my dad's choice in protecting our family's privacy. But the flip side was that people were confused and annoyed by the wedding cancellation.

Of the twenty or so people who knew what happened, very few gave us grace once Rania was home. They were understanding when she was gone, but once she was home, we were expected to have the wedding go on. That is just the mentality of that community. The show must go on. But that did not happen.

Chapter Seven

Disloyalty

After the wedding was canceled, Veer had the nerve to show up at the house.

Chief Ramon had released him upon my dad's request. He still had my dad's car. It still vexes me at his overconfidence and his assumptions that he had any right to come to our home ever again. The audacity to even come inside at that, although he clearly saw my parents, visibility still upset. I felt like they were afraid of him. Once inside, he lacked the simple wisdom and restraint to take the hospitality that was reluctantly given to him, he was aware of this adversity, he knew what happened! Still, he dared to sit down and wanted to talk like nothing happened. Nevertheless, what he dared to ask was appalling.

He declared that he was *taking* Rania with him to New York! I saw my father's reaction and I thought he was ready to punch Veer. Looking back, I commend him for how well he controlled his emotions that day.

The Ungracious Daughter

Not so much for his brothers though. My male cousins had to hold them back in the kitchen as they were ready to 'beat him up."

What was devastating though, was when Rania suddenly got up and announced that indeed, she was leaving with Veer. "I am leaving with him, regardless of what you say. I am an adult, and this is what I want," she claimed. The commotion was on the brink of becoming violent. It was a tumultuous, agitated, noisy commotion that could be heard throughout the entire neighborhood. Everyone was staring at her in shock. That's when my dad lost his composure! His voice roared!

He demanded to know why Rania thought she could leave with this "scamp."

I had never seen my dad so angry. His muscles hardened and contracted. It was obvious that he was restraining from hitting Veer. His veins flattened up against the surface of his skin and appear to bulge at his neck. Yet, Rania was so adamant and stubbornly unyielding. She didn't seem afraid of dad at all. She vowed that she loved Veer and wanted to live with him in New York City. Then she boldly grabbed Veer's hand and walked out the door! Leaving everyone stunned in astonishment and shock.

It was the saddest thing to see my parents watch as Rania walked out of the house and got in the car with Veer. She did not even look back once. We all stood on the veranda, still in shock. My mom, dad, uncles, aunts, and us girls, and watched as she drove off with Veer. He was smiling, almost sneering, and to me, he looked like the typical villain.

My heart sank as I watched my parents. I know she only drove off five minutes ago, but I had the sinking feeling that it was the first step on a faraway trail. Yes, they did try to persuade her to stay, and amongst all the fears and concerns, all the unknowns of this unscrupulous Veer, all they wanted her to do was say no to him and stay home.

That evening, the house felt like someone had died.

Disloyalty

My parents were astounded for hours. It was the ultimate harsh blow any parents would have to deal with. Throughout that intense argument, and even to this day, I wondered why Rania embarked on this weird love affair with Veer. It was understandable that Rania wanted to break free from a boring life, maybe she was unhappy in a mundane existence. I know she was attracted to Veer, but their attraction aside, Veer was a psychopath and kidnapper! How was she not seeing that? That was fixated in my head. Of course, my overemotional and melodramatic brain, had me wondering if Rania was getting attracted to the villain traits of Veer, and that was a turn-on for her. That she would eventually embrace the darkness within, and she too will become a villain. Like Bonnie and Clyde.

Scott chuckled.
Don't laugh, Maya remarked. But even she thought her remark was funny.

I have seen it so many times in movies where the victim gets attracted to their kidnapper. Years later, I found out that it is called Stockholm Syndrome, where the victim grows positive feelings toward the captors or abusers. They develop negative feelings toward police or other authority figures. The victims then sympathize with their captor's beliefs and behaviors. I believe this may have happened to Rania.

Rania had never had a boyfriend or felt wanted or loved by a man before, and so her feelings were typical, because of the emotional and highly charged situation she was in, during being held hostage.

Most often people who are kidnapped or taken hostage, often feel threatened by their captors, but they are also highly reliant on them for survival. What she must have felt was not love, it was merely lust and attraction.

However, the sheer embarrassment and shame on my parents did not end there. What happened the next day, I will never forget it as long as I live.

Maya felt a sudden sadness for her parents. Her face contorted and she shook her head and wept. Scott sensed the sadness in her voice as she tried to continue. He held her close.

The Ungracious Daughter

"You don't have to talk about this if it is too painful," He spoke.
"No, I want to continue." So she did.

The next day was another blow to mom and dad's devastation and distress. I thought for sure this was going to destroy and shatter them. That morning, mom and dad were sitting on the settee, dad pretending to read the newspaper, yet I noticed how edgy and distracted he was. Mom was hemming some pieces of fabric. Us girls, were just sitting around on the living room couch, not talking, too distressed and distraught from the past few days to even bother to be tormented by any small talk or conversation. The atmosphere was noiseless and gloomy. This was rare in a house filled with girls.

A white Honda Civic pulled up on the parapet, in front of our house.

Dad looked down from where he was sitting and let up an inaudible sound. We all ran to the verandah door, just in time to see Veer stepping out of the car, removing his Ray-Ban sunglasses, and giving a bright, wide smile at my dad. His white teeth gleamed in the sunlight. Then Rania got out, wearing a long white skirt and a white 'float over' lace blouse, and white strap-heel sandals. Her long dark hair, flowing around her shoulders. She looked haughty, almost arrogant. Yet, beautiful at the same time.

Then the realization of what was happening hit my dad like a bullet struck his chest, sucking the breath out of him. He fell back in his chair shocked, stunned at what was happening.

Following right behind Rania and Veer, in a police cruiser, were two police officers!

"The Police! But is that not your mom's uncle?" Scott exclaimed.

Yes, but there was nothing he could do, as Rania made a report that her belongings were being held and she wanted an escort to get her passport and her things. She said she was too afraid to come alone or even with Veer, as my uncles had threatened him. The police had no choice but to come with her. Her actions were callous, heartless, and unfeeling. She did not have to do that. My parents would have given her everything that belonged to her.

My mother would have never wanted her to go without her belongings. Although she never worked a day in her life, and everything was bought by my parents, they would have given it to her without any restrictions or hesitation.

Veer walked across the street and watched from the Tailor's shop. He must have been too afraid to get beat up, I guess. I thought he was just a coward, letting Rania do the dirty work, showing up with the police to get her belongings, from my parent's home. That was so devastating and shameful and unbelievable. To this day, I cannot come to terms with the fact that she brought the police!

Rania's dramatic duplicity and betrayal and Veer's actions had them on the run now. When my uncles found out, mere hours later, they threatened to get him. It was believed that Veer and Rania ended up in the creek again, trying to hide out there before fleeing to New York. Mom and Dad consulted with Chief Ramon but there was nothing he could do to stop Rania from leaving with Veer. She was nineteen and considered an adult.

Days later, law enforcement arrived at our home again, confirming that they had left for New York.

In my head, I still could not understand what her plans were. Sure, she was in love with Veer, but she had no permanent status in New York, and Veer couldn't sponsor her if he was married already. What were her plans? Was she going to live there illegally? I overheard dad saying to mom, 'I'm a strong person, so why am I having such a difficult time getting past Rania's betrayal?' This was so sad to hear, as my dad is not one to open up and talk about his feelings. It broke my heart. I believe it to be a reason for me agreeing to an arranged marriage years later.

Rania's estrangement was affecting everyone in the house. There were so many unanswered questions. Both my parent's reactions were similar. A sense of betrayal is one of the most profound wounds felt by parents of adult, estranged children. How could their child, to whom they had given so much love and energy, turn their back so readily, and without any feelings? The betrayal and rejection my parents felt were profound.

The foundation they thought was solid, felt more like quicksand as they began to question themselves, their relationship with their children, and their parenting. What have their lives been all about? Where do they go from here? What does the future hold for them now? Would they have to live with a broken heart forever, dealing with the estrangement of their eldest daughter?

Years later, when I asked my parents to describe the relationship before the rift, they said they maintained it out of "moral obligation." Mom said that as Rania grew into a teenager, she never felt close to her anymore. She was distant, reserved and kept to herself.

When asked whether they bear some responsibility for the estrangement, they both said yes. Rania, on the other hand, was much harsher in her reflection of the whole situation, and never really want to talk about it. She impassively told me 'I do not want to talk about the past, but I will say they still see me as a child. They still have difficulty giving up that paradigm. They don't see me as an adult. Also, we don't have the same values. We never did, but they did not see that. They chose to see what they wanted to and ignore everything else about me, and you too for that matter. Even as an adult, when I make choices that aren't consistent with their values, they would say, 'We didn't raise you that way.' They have trouble acknowledging that grown children are responsible for developing their own moral compasses."

Maya stopped here, she had to. She did not want to tell Scott the rest of the story, right before going over to Daya and Assam's, knowing that the entire family would be there. She did not want any uneasiness. She

Disloyalty

needed to take a break from the story, she had to prepare to let go of the emotions before facing everyone that evening.

The evening was wonderful. Music, drinks, delicious food, and great company. Scott got along so well with Assam, from the first time they met, it was as if they had known each other since birth. The family jokes that they are brothers from another mother and since Maya met Scott, Assam stopped BBQing, even at his own home, as Scott was 'the grill master."

The men were playing dominoes after dinner, as the women chatted. Maya, her sisters, daughters, and nieces were discussing plans for costumes for the dance school. This is always exciting for them. She looked over at Scott, who had picked up the game quickly, and smiled. She knew he would be shocked at the next chapters of the story. Yet, he had to know. Maya looked at Daya and wondered how she would feel about Maya disclosing her disappearance, to Scott. It was something that was never talked about again in the family.

Chapter Eight

The Executioner

The next day Maya must have slept in. She opened her eyes to find Scott beside the bed staring down at her lovingly.
"Well, well well, look who finally decide to open her eyes."

She said nothing. As Scott spoke, she realized that she had a headache. Must be all that wine the night before, she thought.
Scott plopped down on the bed next to her. The motion made the headache worse.
'What time is it," she asked weakly.
"Almost noon," Scott said and laughed. "Do I get points for letting you sleep in?"
"Noon," she repeated. "I need to get up and shower, you will get lots of kisses after, and that's your points."

She took two aspirin and went into the shower.

The Ungracious Daughter

Brunch that day was one of her favorite Guyanese leftovers. Dhal puri they had brought home from the BBQ, with fried eggs, green onions and wiri-wiri pepper. The headache was gone shortly after she ate, making her realize that it was caused by hunger. They both settle down in the sunroom again, knowing that the rest of the narrative had to be told.

Maya continued.

Overwhelmed after not hearing from Rania, my parents never gave up hope. But moving back into normalcy, days after the wedding cancellation, the kidnapping, the trauma of their daughter's betrayal, was far too difficult. There were so many questions and inquiries from other family members and friends. Keep in mind that mom was in the 'Mahila Mandalee' and all her upscale friends were very inquisitive. I always thought they were nosy, arrogant, stuck-up socialites.

Rania's leaving and the devastating fact that she was willing to go with Veer even though he was lying, and even almost committed bigamy, left mom and dad distraught, embarrassed, and ashamed to even step outside. Mom was agitated and riddled with doubts and mental conflict. It was painful to see her like this. She was not eating, sleeping, or working. We had never seen her not working. Daya and I were so worried about mom, who was becoming increasingly distressed.

After this horrible ordeal, none of us wanted to even be seen by the neighbors, so we kept indoors.

This morning was no different. Daya left early. As she got into her car that was parked in our car port below the house, I put the dogs back in the kennel. They were watchdogs and we kept them in the kennel during the day. I waved at her as she drove out of the driveway, not knowing the events of that day would change our lives forever.

That evening, I made dinner. I was just learning to cook, and I made chicken chowmein, thinking it may cheer everyone up as it was a usual winner. By dinner time, Daya had not returned from work, which was unusual. She was always home by 5:30pm or she would let us know if she had to work late. Upon calling the office, mom was told that she had left in the morning with a pile of documents, saying she would work at home that day.

This sent us into a spiral of events that led us to a hitman.

"Hitman?! Scott was jolted as Maya continued as if it was normal to talk about a hitman.

Yes, as crazy as it sounds, I will never forget it. His name was Max. I assumed it was short for Maximilian. Since then, I have always associated that name with villains, ever since. I remembered the hitman's story to the police very clearly as if it was yesterday.

Daya's disappearance immediately prompted Chief Ramon and his team to search for Veer's whereabouts after she failed to return home. They even pulled Assam in for questioning. Mom and Dad had an inclination that Daya and Assam liked eachother and she may have run away with him for fear they won't agree to the relationship.

I was the one who answered the phone when Max called.

Don't hang up, he said as if reading my thoughts because there were so many people calling to tell us they knew where she was. Just hear me out, he said. I know where your sister is, although she may not be alive.

I felt a feeling of terror and anguish.

"Where is she? Where is she?" I demanded.

He was silent for what seemed to be an eternity.

Then he quietly said, "I would say right where your other sister was."

"But where is she," I kept asking.

The Ungracious Dauther

Max told me what Veer had planned for Daya. He had told Max that he was going to handle it himself. That was 13 hours earlier when Max called to tell him he could not do the job.

He had said it so coldly, I don't think he realized that our phone was tapped because he was speaking very slowly as if he had all the time in the world. I answered, "But where is that?" my voice was trembling as though threatened by tears when he said that. I felt my body was perilously close to getting sucked into a conversation that I was not prepared to handle.

But then the line went dead.

I know that the detectives were listening. They made notes as Max gave the details. Most of them took off quickly. Two were going to pick up Max. The others left to find Daya where Max thought she might be.

Chief Ramon quickly questioned me about the conversation. He didn't speak to me as other adults did, he didn't act like I was a child, but talked as if I was a grown-up. Initially, it was a surprise to me, but by then I was already 16, and he must have recognized that. I was visibly shaking but had to relay my conversation with Max.

Scott was appalled at Maya's story. His heart ached as Maya looked up at him. He stared at her lovingly as she give him a weak smile. "How did they find her?" he finally asked. He knew this must have been dreadful for Maya. She and Daya are very close.

Max helped us to find her. He was arrested near the main police station in Georgetown. It was so easy as if he wanted to be caught.

He confessed to Chief Ramon. He recounted everything, his feelings, his words, and his actions.

Veer had come to his apartment. Max had done some small jobs for Veer back in the 80s, but he had not seen or heard from him for several years after the last job in Trinidad. Veer had returned to the United States.

The Executioner

But even for those other jobs, Veer had never come to Max's place before. His usual correspondence was by a third party. This must be big. Max recalled that Veer looked tired and older than his usual boyish self.

Veer followed him into his apartment and shut the door. Max's first reaction was to ask what the heck he was doing there. Veer asked him to relax. It's not as if he had never seen him before, although it had been a long time.

Veer explained his plans to Max. He kept saying that someone had to be held accountable for him having to hide out in the creek and for rumors that his own mother was dead. It was apparent that Veer will go to murderous lengths to get to Daya, the woman he blames for the rumors of his mother being dead. The revulsion of finding out that people thought his mother was dead was unbearable. He has sworn vengeance against Daya long ago. Determined to bring her to his absurd idea of justice, Veer's next step was to hire Max to "take care" of her.

Veer knew that Max was the biggest hitman in Georgetown. He had done jobs for him before. Jobs that were too dangerous for Veer to do himself. Max was skillful, quick-witted, and nimble and got the job done fast and with ease, almost effortlessly. Regardless of the challenges, Max managed to gather the essential facts of the job. Veer had a prime job for him, the biggest that Veer ever asked for. She is the Office Manager of Timer Lumber.

As soon as Max heard it was Timer Lumber, he told Veer it was a waste of time. There was heavy security there, and Max expressed these concerns and the fact that the entire premises were usually cordoned off with barbed wire and roads in its precinct had heavy security presence. The only people that were allowed to enter the small roads leading to the massive building, were the ones working there or you had to have an appointment, which was hard to come by.

I remembered going in to see Daya at work once, or even accompanying her sometimes on the weekends. Due to the time difference when she had to send documents to Germany. I remembered every time I went there, the extravagant lobby never ceased to amaze me.

On the outside, the building looked like older colonial structures in Georgetown, but then you enter into a foyer that could accommodate the extremely large Areca palm plant, at the foot of a vast curving staircase, that seemed like it went to heaven. Polished wood floors and a graceful banister that curved up toward a soaring second-floor gallery, led to the offices. Imported Persian rugs covered the entire hallway.

Danny Singh spared no expenses. I was always in awe of their extravagance and lavish taste. Danny was Premika's cousin.

Anyway, getting back to Max's story.

Veer assured Max not to worry. He knew how to get him into the compound. He had a VIP pass from months before that Daya had arranged for Veer when he came to show her the engagement ring. Veer said the security did not even check the date on it.

Max thought it was the ideal setup, but he was eager to find out what this big job was. Veer got right down to it without wasting any time.
"I need you to get rid of her." Max recalled Veer taking out a photo from his briefcase. His immediate reaction was wow, what a very pretty woman. He was always attracted to Indian women with dark curly hair.
 "Any ideas about who the lucky lady is?" He asked Max.
"She is my fiancé's sister," Veer replied.
"Your fiancé. Did you get a divorce? Aren't you married," he asked Veer.
"It's a long story," Veer told him. Max recalled asking Veer how the heck he was supposed to get out of there after the job was done. Veer said that Max had to wait for the evening when Daya was leaving. She always parked at the far side of the lot. Veer had recalled her saying that was her daily exercise.

Max said that night, he could not sleep, so he decided to work out. The noise of the treadmill was a steady hum under his feet. He must have

The Executioner

walked for more than an hour before hitting the showers. He felt a sense of dread, as if he was connected to this woman somehow. Max explained that he had never felt like this for any of his targets before. Still, he could not sleep after the workout. He turned on the music. It was blaring in the apartment, but it still wasn't enough to drone out his thoughts of that beautiful woman, so he turned the music louder, glad that his apartment was soundproof. He recalled that he kept on going at a frantic pace. He had gone over all the options and plans in the dark of the night, coming up with several ideas, but none seemed to lead to this woman getting out alive.

By the next morning, he had a plan, a relatively simple plan. He would walk in there and tell her the truth.

The next day, Max went to Timer Lumber, pretending to be working on a lumber sales project.

He drove up to the security, and as Veer predicted, the security only quickly glanced at his VIP pass and let him through. Max thought to himself, why the heavy security and no one checking, but who was he to wonder how they were doing their jobs? He was in. That was all that mattered.

Max walked up to the reception confidently. The older woman there was quite friendly, and Max told her he had an appointment with Mr. Danny Singh, the owner. She checked her binder and could not find him on the calendar.

Nevertheless, she made a quick call and explain that there was a potential buyer who wanted to see Mr. Singh.

Shortly after, Max was escorted by a young woman wearing high heels up the winding staircase to the long lavishly designed boardroom. She told him that Mr. Singh's assistant would be right there. Max was sweating bullets by then, his palms felt clammy. His nervousness was apparent.

There was a knock on the door and then she came in. Miss Daya entered, placing a fresh cup of coffee on a desk. "Mr. Mac, can I get you anything else."

The Ungracious Daughter

"It is Max," he recalled saying. He didn't want anything, not even the coffee. Max is not usually nervous, but then again, he had never had to tell an innocent young woman that her life was in danger.

Her bright brown eyes gleamed under long lashes. She had shoulder-length dark curly hair, just like in the picture, her skin was hazel, and she was professionally dressed, in a white lace shirt, black skirt, and a black blazer buttoned at the waist. Max remembered thinking that she could do with some sleep to get rid of the dark circles under her eyes, and maybe eat more. She was pencil thin. I suppose in this case it doesn't matter now, he had thought to himself. What mattered was what needed to be done. Damn, my life is fucked, he thought to himself. The words could not come. He tired to stall.

He told Daya he is waiting for Mr. Danny Singh. She nodded, turned around, exited the boardroom, and closed the door behind her. Max remembered getting up from the chair and unbuttoning the top of his shirt. He was profusely sweating now, as he looked out of the floor-length glass windows that overlooked a lush green garden.

He had not been so nervous since his early days.

He remembered thinking, how am I going to tell her that her brother-in-law was behind this? What if they arrested him right there and then? Chief Ramon would be thrilled, Max thought. He wanted Max so badly but never had charges that were laid on Max, to stick. Max had friends in high places.

Max's thoughts were interrupted when Miss Daya returned and indicated that Mr. Singh was in a meeting and won't be able to see him until after one hour. That pretty girl is someone's sister, someone's daughter. Fuck. What did you get yourself into Max...? This is serious, and fucked, he remembered thinking.

I have to tell her the truth, I have to tell her what Veer wanted me to do, but how? Max was feeling so nervous he can feel it down his spine.

"Listen! Miss, your life is in danger!" he blurted. Daya had looked at him as if he was ill.
"Are you okay," she asked him. Her voice was raspy and confused. "Mr. Mac, can I help you?"

He didn't answer but looked at her with intensity. This was not someone that he could easily get rid of. He looked at her and knew that she did not deserve this, her family did not deserve this, and he had to tell her the truth.
"I am! But you are not! You need to go home; you need to find a safe place."
She made a strange sound. He ignored it, wanting to make sure she understood what was happening.
"Do you have anyone to take you home?"
She shook her head, yes. He told her to lock her office and take an early lunch.
"But why, why am I in danger?" she asked. Max was bewildered by her bravery.
"It's Veer! He wants you dead! After what you said about his mother."
Reality sank in for Miss Daya. Her heart sank, in the realization of what was happening, as she dropped into the black leather chair. Max quickly left. His quick departure only emphasized the fact that she was in danger.

Max's story continued.

What the fuck did I do, Max recalled. Max knew he had to see Veer.

He had to tell him that he could not be his 'hit man' any longer. Max showed up at Veer's sister's house.
Veer was appalled that Max would show up here. He grabbed Max by the shirt and shoved him into the side stairwell.
"What the fuck, asshole."
"Where is she?" Max asked Veer, what have you done? I heard her family is looking for her. What the fuck, Veer!"
Max paced around in circles, facing him and then they squared off. Veer had his hands up and began to circle slowly, almost dancing around Max.

The Ungracious Daughter

He was cocky, he chose a few test punches and Max reacted slowly. "Come on Veer," Max recalled saying. He stared at Veer, but he seemed patient. Max tried to throw a short punch and pulled it back in and then did a spinning back kick that connected with Veer's midsection hard.

It looked like Veer was hurt, but Max threw some more skillful punches and kicks. Veer seems to be growing impatient now, he went in for Max's head, hard, but he was waiting for this, and sidesteps with surprising speed and blocks the attack, and sent a brutal kick. Veer landed on the ground, face down. Max panicked. He ran, got into his car, and left. Max said that he hoped that the two of them would never see each other or talk about "that poor girl" ever again. They never heard from each other again. Yet Max knew he had to tell her family, they had to know.

Scott rubbed his eyes, still in disbelief. He stood up and stared down at Maya, who seemed lost in her thoughts. Maya's memories of when Daya went missing were still painfully fresh in her mind. She had never really gotten over the fact that her two older sisters were at the mercy of Veer, this horrible callous, unemotional, and morally depraved man.

It was days before Daya even spoke after she was found. She was immediately taken to St. Joseph's Hospital and stayed there for two days, while questioned by the Chief and detectives, but it was days later she recounted the horrifying ordeal. Before that horrific day, Daya remembered a man coming to her office to warn her about Veer. She was scared and left the office immediately, but trouble would find Daya on that horrible day, as she'd meet a monster in the parking lot. She recalled her ordeal with Veer. Her fear that he would kill her. She would never forget that evil look in his eyes.

Daya recalled that after Max warned her that her life was in danger, she went to look for Assam to take her home, but he was in Mr. Singh's office for a financial meeting, so she left immediately, with some very important work she had to finish that day. She told the receptionist that she was going home and remembered walking nervously to her car.

The Executioner

Daya strode towards her car. She had parked in the last row of the expansive parking lot. She wished she could get out of this habit of parking at the end of the lot. It was lonely in this area. She shifted the stack of documents, she held in her arms, to a more comfortable position, almost tripping on the curb while she did so. She recovered from her stumbled and continued walking. She reached in her purse, searching for her keys, only to whip her hand out again, to save the pile of documents. Why was the pile so irritatingly large? She reached for her keys again.

Then she felt a sharp pain in her head.

She wondered why everything was getting so bright. It was almost like a set of flashlights were being shined straight into her eyes. Then the pain came, and in the same moment, it was gone, her body now lay there in the middle of the parking lot.

Years later, Rania recounted how Veer relayed his sinister accomplishments. He had never talked about this before, always denying that he had anything to do with Daya's disappearance. After eight years of isolation, and no contact made with her family, he knew she could be trusted.
She was his, body, soul, and mind. She never once tried to disobey him. He knew she was not going to do anything to jeopardize the relationship. She loved him too much for that. One night, after several glasses of red wine, he confided in Rania. This is what he told Rania.
It was midnight, the sky was dark, and the streets were deserted. Veer's favourite time of the day. Most people were already asleep in the quiet countryside in Mahaica creek. Like Daya was, in the dingy room at the end of the hallway. He smiled, thinking how little she knew that her real nightmare was about to begin. He laughed.

What did she think, he was going to let her get away with claiming his mother was dead! He imagined what he would do to her. He imagined her shaking her head at him in disdain. She never liked him.

He had a plan for her. He had taken a moment to admire the leanness of his physique. The hardness of his biceps beneath the white cotton shirt.

He had always taken great care with his appearance and at thirty-four, he could easily pass for twenty-five. He was proud of his good looks.

He shook his head and walked into the dining kitchen area, adjoining the living room, and looked towards the bedroom. He had to finish what Max couldn't do. He thought of grabbing a beer, before heading down the hallway but changed his mind. He wanted a clear head for this. He opened the bedroom door. He could make out her small shape under the floral sheet, her hip protruding through the thin fabric. He made sure earlier that she was naked under the sheet. Not that he was interested in her that way, she was far too thin and small-breasted for his taste. He preferred his women softer, meatier, and more vulnerable. He looked at her thin frame and smiled. It was part of his intimidation and his need to shame her. If only she had learned to keep that big mouth shut. Maybe this would not be happening to her. Everything that would happen to her that night, was her fault.

He recalled how he just wanted to leave her there in Mahaica creek, for days but knew he had to get the show on the road. He had to get out of the country soon after this.

He remembered slipping his hands into his pocket and feeling the hardness of the knife's handle against his fingers. He always liked that feeling. That feeling of control and dominance. He lowered himself on the bed, his hip grazing hers, as the springs of the old mattress squeaked.

"Wakey wakey, Daya," he had whispered in her ear. "Time to wake up and smell the coffee."
He wondered if she was dead already. That would be fun. Then Daya let out a low moan but didn't move.
"Wake up bitch," he shouted. Both his hands were around her frail neck. Her eyes shot open.

"What the heck are you doing?" she demanded.

Veer said he just wanted to snap her neck right there and be done with it. He had sensed her defiance creeping in the corners of her voice. He

The Executioner

loosened his grip. She slipped from under him and made a run for the door, screaming at the top of her lungs for someone to hear, and come rescue her. He recalled in amusement how he watched her reach for the door, knowing he had plenty of time before she would be able to open the door. She certainly was courageous, he recalled, not without admiration.

And pretty strong for a skinny girl. He had no intention of slitting her throat. No, that would be too messy. Not to mention unnecessarily risky since Chief Ramon was already looking for him. He had decided she needed to pay for what she said about his mother, before he and Rania left for the US. She was kicking and screaming as he grabbed her by the throat again. His fingers tightened around her. He had to use his hands; it was the cleanest way. He could easily drop her in the creek before they took off. Even after her arms went limp at her sides, when he was certain that she was dead, he held on to her neck for another full minute, silently counting the seconds before releasing his fingers. He remembered smiling with satisfaction as her body collapsed at his feet. He lifted Daya's warm body and placed it back on the bed. She looked at him with cold eyes. He was certain she was dead.

When Daya told her story, she recalled that everything seemed to happen at once. She vaguely recalled lying in the parking lot for what seemed like an eternity, when someone picked her up and placed her in a vehicle. The next thing she knew, Veer was shouting in her ear, then she was awake and screaming as she struggled to get up. The horrible ache in her head was getting worse, Veer's continuous shouting assaults her ears.

She looked around and did not recognize where she was. Veer was straddled over her, sneering, a shiny knife in his hand. She jumped off the bed and was racing wildly around the room, looking for the door. Veer reached for her; his hand reached out to silence her. Her screams turned to whimpers beneath the pressure of his hand. She grasped for air, as he lifted her effortlessly with one arm and pinned her to the wall by the door.

"Are you going to shut up," he barked? She shut up and stared at him in disbelief. "Surprised to see me?" he asked her. Her eyes darted to the door. He sensed she was thinking to make a run for it.

"I think you need to get that thought out of your head, you don't want to make me angry."

His eyes were an evil shade of steel gray. He pinned her to the door, his fingers wrapping tightly around her neck.

"Where am I, what am I doing here?" she asked him, fearing the answer. She wouldn't let him see her fear.

"You asked for this bitch. I don't want to do it, but you are making me do this.'
His fingers squeezing, choking. She could not breathe. She felt a sharp pain in her stomach and remembered him loosening his grip as she slips to the floor. Everything went dark.

Daya's only recollection after that was looking up at Chief Ramon's gentle smile as he carried her out to the police car, lights flashing everywhere. Veer was long gone.

I always liked Uncle Ramon. He was a clean-cut and organized man, known for slipping dollars to me and Nadia for getting A's on our report cards. He was also incredibly punctual and was known to be the man who bought all the best liquor for our family events.

So, how did they find her? Scott demanded. He seemed to be a little exasperated that Maya was talking about some uncle, while he was sitting on bricks, waiting to know what happen next.

They found her! Exactly where Max predicted! Unconscious! In the small hut in Mahaica creek!

It's the walk every policeman dread, deep into the dark woods in search of a body, led there by a suspected killer who not only told them where to find the victim but who attempted to kill her.

Police cars were rolling up as they searched through the tangled overgrowth to a clearing, where the small hut was, and in there, the body of Daya was found, unconscious, and left for dead. But in this shocking tale of terror, everything changes in the blink of an eye.

Veer is a criminal as callous as they come. Not only did he attempt to snap Daya's neck and leave her for dead – but hours later, he left the country as if nothing had happened.

The irony of it all is that Veer was never charged with attempted murder or kidnapping. He was gone!
Hours later, with Rania! Around the same time that Max was in custody for questioning, mom and dad received a letter, addressed to dad only, hand delivered by a young boy who claimed that a man and a woman (Veer's and Rania's description) give him twenty US dollars to hand-delivered a letter at 10:00 pm that night. No later, no earlier.

The note read:

> Listen carefully Bali, your daughter has decided to leave with me and there's nothing you can do. She's an adult and it is her choice. I am not holding her hostage or doing her any harm. But know that I'm not playing here either. Don't try anything, let us leave peacefully and maybe you can hear from her when we get where we are going. Any deviation from my instructions will be an immediate cut-off from your daughter. You will be denied her whereabouts and any contact with her. Do not provoke me or speak to anyone about this situation, such as your good friend Chief Ramon. It would only result in your daughter never being heard from again. If we catch you talking to even a stray dog, or if you alert the authorities before we leave, you will not hear from her. Don't try to grow a brain now Bali. Do not underestimate me. Use that good common sense of yours!
>
> Your loving son-in-law,
> Veer

This was devastating and demoralizing to mom and dad. Their whole world had turned upside down. All that they worked so hard to build, their prestige, their image, and their respect in society, have all gone, taken by Veer. My family's image is now going down the drain, because of this imbecile, or as my dad called him, nincompoop. Worse of all, Dad nearly lost two daughters at the hands of Veer, and he is not even sure if one is still alive.

Sadly, my dad asked Chief Ramon to drop any pending charges on Veer or Max. He wanted to keep peace with Veer, for fear of not hearing from Rania or ever seeing her again. He was afraid that Veer would harm her. Both mom and dad felt that Rania was being held against her will, but I never believed that.

I always felt she played a big part in all of the betrayal and deceit.

Maya paused, reflecting on this horrible ordeal.

Scott asked, "But did they leave for the US?"

We did not know at the time. Chief Ramon did go to the airport immediately but unfortunately, it was too late when he found out that they had left before the letter was delivered. Although the detectives were staking out at the airport, we believe either Veer bribed the airport officials, or they left in disguise or with fake passports. We still do not know what happened. To this day Rania claims that she was drugged and does not recall any of what happened or how she got to America.

Maya was done. Her emotions frayed. She could no longer talk about anything. That evening they went out with their friends for dinner and a movie at the Shops of Don Mills in Toronto. It was an early evening as the next day everyone had to get back to work after the long weekend.

Chapter Nine

Missing in Action

That entire week, Maya was emotional. Recounting all the hidden memories and trauma that had taken a toll on her. She could not sleep. These memories she would have rather kept forgotten. They triggered emotions and feelings that she was not prepared to handle. Ryder and Sean sensed it as soon as she came home. She knew that she had to get it over with and tell Scott everything else, once and for all.

The following weekend, they got into a routine: wake up, have breakfast, sit in the sunroom and talk. Break for snacks and dinner but everything needed to be told, no holding back. Maya picked up from where she left off the weekend before.

Life went on for us. We never heard from Rania. We were not even sure if she was indeed living in New York City. For years, the horror stories my mom and dad heard about Rania in New York were unbelievable and shocking. They were told that she was in pornography movies and that people saw her in prostitution, but we never heard from her, not for eight years. The people that started these rumors are just despicable as Veer. Maybe it was his family that started those awful rumors, just to get back at us.

The fact that my parents had not heard from Rania would suggest that some serious issues need to be resolved. Yet, how can they get resolved if we did not even know where she was or even if she is alive? The uncertainty was painful.

They were estranged from Rania for so long. The experience and ambiguity about the relationship's future, left them feeling like their lives were on hold. They found themselves in a sort of limbo between the past and the uncertain future.

Dad stopped playing in the band, mom kept away from most of her social groups.

They were embarrassed and ashamed.

Maya looked at Scott. She thought about her children and how they have to go back and forth every other weekend to visit their dad and grandparents.

At first, my father was also devastated, and sadly, he turned his pain of abandonment to anger. Since Daya worked, Nadia and I were in school, and we were both stuck having to be the 'care-taker.' Mom and Dad were on two different pages and I was the one they both talked to, not each other. I had to be the strong one. I was angry and resentful. When Rania left with the police, none of us knew enough at the time to truly grasp the immense gravity of the act. It should have been a big red flag that something was wrong, but none of us got it.

When Rania first went missing, I was so worried and sad. Was she abused too? Is that why she is trying to make my parents pay for this?

Missing in Action

The emotional impact is significant. The term "living in limbo" is often used to describe how families can't move on while a loved one is missing. They often fluctuate between hope and hopelessness. I began to analyze the situation, in my head, possibly that she was dead, though I found it odd that a mother wouldn't know by instinct if her child was dead. I tried to be calm and philosophical and told myself that this was all just a big mistake. This is not happening, stop panicking, there is a logical explanation, and she will come waltzing through the door. But deep down I knew something was wrong, and it was terrifying.

As parents, protecting our kids from pain comes naturally. The bottom line is, we can't control our child's actions. Regret, guilt, or any other emotion was evident in mom and dad's demeanor. In the beginning, they started to ponder various what-if scenarios. What if we moved abroad? What if our estranged daughter did not find out that we may move to the US or Canada? She'll regret not reaching out to us earlier. And then there was the other extreme. What if a death occurs? What if she waits until it's too late? She will suffer guilt.

The more they speculated on what-ifs, the more they got caught up in feeling. Feeling things about scenarios that hadn't even occurred, and ones they couldn't control anyway.
After a few years, they started to work through the negative thoughts. I think they started to believe that they could handle not knowing how it would all turn out.
They eventually started to switch to something more positive. I remember Mom saying to dad "I don't like not knowing, but I can accept it for now. This isn't what I expected to happen, but it's tolerable."
There were no giant leaps at joy and positivity. It was just realistic steps in the right direction.
They both knew that life's roads are not smooth or without bumps and detours. With support, encouragement from family members, and the passage of time, they started a plan to secure a better life and future in Canada. Those arrangements had to be accelerated quicker than originally planned.

The Ungracious Daughter

You may remember me telling you that my dad was in the government opposition party, and he was also the Public Heath Prosecutor in court. The political parties were always referred to as left and right. The terms left and right are used to describe the two main different political parties, the People's Progressive Party (PPP) and People's National Congress (PNC). The left side of the spectrum is the People's Progressive Party (PPP) which involved mostly the Indian population of Guyana. On the other hand, the People's National Congress included mostly the African population of Guyana. For generations, they fought with each other.

My dad was one of the leaders who coordinated a peaceful declaration for a strike asking the government to give the power back to the people from the PNC after rigged elections. This strike did not go well and triggered several political protests, riots, and violence. My dad became one of the most targeted persons in the opposition party. One night, coming home from a walk with my mom, he was brutally attacked.

The attack began with the assailant approaching dad saying that he knew him from the court, and then offering out his hand for a handshake. When dad obliged his request for a handshake, the attacker then refused to let go, proceeding to throw dad to the ground, before kicking him and stomping on his head. All the while, my mother screamed for help.

Once dad appeared unconscious, the assailant searched his pockets, stealing various items, all of which were of no value, leaving his gold watch intact on his wrist. Among the stolen items were $500 in cash, his wallet and his driver's license.

Dad's left eye was severely damaged, and he was spitting up blood. Weeks later, and he was still suffering from severe headaches and had to be off work for several weeks. During that time, a neighbor came in the backdoor of our house to let my father know soldiers were coming to our home. My dad ran out of the back door as the soldiers walked to the front. The soldiers searched the house, and terrorized my mother, before they left with a warning that they would kill her if they could not find my dad.

Missing in Action

After a couple of weeks, a newspaper was published listing all the men and women who left government positions, which included my dad's and his close friends' names. Four days later he secretly left for the US. Still trying to stay positive and move forward. He was forced into leaving his government position, because he knew that he needed to if he wanted his family to survive. He was forced to put his selfishness aside for the survival of himself and his family and was willing to do whatever it took. He was forced to leave the country.

When my dad left for the US, it was even worse, as my mom had never been apart from him, and her loneliness and sadness became even more profound.

Chapter Ten

Unexpected Encounter

Dad saw Rania for the first time at the New York subway station.

I remembered the day clearly when dad called us, to tell us that he met Rania on the train. Dad usually calls on Saturday evenings, on his weekends in Connecticut. He worked there on weekends and his boss used to let him call home, long-distance, free of charge. This particular day was a Tuesday. We had just come home from school, early, as we were experiencing a tropical storm with very powerful thunder and lightning. There were strong winds and heavy rainfall, and it was disruptive to the phone lines. We could not hear dad very well. We barely caught something about Rania and the subway. Before getting disconnected for the umpteenth time. We heard Dad promising to write us, to explain what happened, as he wasn't going to Connecticut for a few weeks. All the following week we were very worried, and Mom could not sleep. I remember stalking the postman to see if he had any letters for us.

When it finally arrived, we all gathered in the front living room and sat around mom, who was on the settee, us girls on the floor. Mom could not even open the envelope, so I took it and opened it. I loved reading Dad's letters. I always thought he was the best writer, very descriptive and explanatory.

I read the letter to my mom and my sisters. I will never forget those words. It broke my heart. I remembered my face was hot with tears. We were all crying, but I stayed strong and read the entire letter.

> *Dear beautiful wife and children:*
>
> *You are the most precious, loveliest, and most important people in my life. This physical distance has become more troublesome than I thought. No matter where I go, I think of you all the time. I love you for life. I cherish every second of our life together, and now that we are apart, I miss you all so much. Premika, this evening, as I write this letter, it is with great pain and difficulty to do what I had to do, without you by my side.*
>
> *Yesterday, I met Rania on the subway train on my way home from Manhattan to Queens. I was not scared or fearful of meeting her. I was fearful that I would have to let her go again. I underestimated the power of the heart, the love of a parent for a child. When I saw Rania stepping out from the shadows, I realized she had seen me first. I was so shocked and yet, tentative, and unsure. Every day, I had hoped to see her, on the train, in the streets of Queens, in the busy streets of Manhattan. It had been one year since I moved here to New York and never ran into her. Every time I see someone that looks like her, my heart races. Yesterday was that fateful day. She wore a face like she was expecting anger from me, anger that just did not exist. All I have for her is love, all I want is to know that she is safe. All I wanted was to let her know that I missed her. That you all missed her and worry about her. But the look on her face told me that she wouldn't accept it just yet, she feels so much misplaced guilt. In truth, it felt like*

she was still such a kid, still growing into her adult body. Then I sensed a look on her face that she wants to own her mistakes, but she needs to forgive herself first. So, I took the emotions that swirled inside of me and put a stopper on them, not to bottle them up forever but instead to keep the love safe until she could accept it as her birthright.

In the split second that she was illuminated by the flickering subway light, my face fell from elation to horror and then to a controlled visage of concern. Though her voice is the same, had I seen her first I would have denied it was her. What was once an innocent face, a child's face, beautiful, like you, Premika, is now that of a mature woman. Still beautiful but changed. Pain and shame were evident.

I know if she was not dubious, I'd be running forward at this point, throwing myself into her arms, but I could not. I stepped forwards, keen that she shouldn't go. After so long, not seeing my eldest daughter, I think I would have just been horrified if she turned away now. I needed her to stay there, to let me hug her, to talk to me, to tell me that she was okay, that she was safe, and all the horror stories we heard about her were just rumours, lies. I realized I was slack jawed, bewildered.

When I tried to speak, my voice faltered into unintelligible croaks. I felt the tears coming down, but I did not care. I wanted to tell her that I love her, but I don't think she would have believed me, and I was afraid it would have sounded hollow. Maybe she's disappointed in me, she doesn't know I never gave up looking for her every day since I came to New York. That I never gave up hope she would find me, that WE never give up hope that she would come home. I moved close enough to touch her, her eyes are the same, still that vulnerable girl from Shell Road - the one who all the boys followed like she was the princess of Georgetown, and she didn't even know it. Then her hand rose silently, despite her doubts, and she touched my hair and then my beard. I wish I had shaved that day, but she didn't seem to mind the stubble.

Then she said, "Goodbye, Dad." I snapped inside, snapped like brittle glass, and felt the shards tearing at my guts. I could not speak, the blood left my face, and I gripped at her coat. She stopped, watching me break right before her eyes. Her face stayed unemotional, but something shifted in her posture. "I'm sorry, dad, I have to go, I can't let Veer know I saw you."

I asked her what she meant by that.

She said that Veer had his son living with them and she takes care of him, she had to get back home so she could pick him up from school. If she is late Veer will not be happy. He wanted her to have nothing to do with us, Premika. He forbade her to ever contact us. Premika, I didn't know that Veer has a son!

Anyway, I hope you don't mind, but I believe I spoke for both of us when I told her that I certainly could understand her struggles with Veer and having to take care of his son. I told her that we understand that, but now that she is on her own, and has her own family, the last thing she needs is our opinion. She already knows how you and I feel about Veer, so driving that point home would only increase the acrimony and distance between us. I told her that we understand that her relationship is already hard enough without the constant disapproval of her parents.

Premika, I think that the best thing we can do is accept the fact that our days of managing our daughter are over and that it's time to learn how to build a relationship with her and that idiot we would have to call son-in-law. He is tenacious and has a very strong hold on her, for whatever reason that is. Just because he put us through such embarrassment, shame, and dishonor and caused our daughter to betray us considerably, and we still do not approve of him for her, we need to accept that it is our daughter's *choice, and it doesn't mean that we can't learn to accept him now that he's a part of our family. I'm not suggesting this will be an easy transition. I know that we all have feelings of resentment and frustration that they both disrespected, betrayed, embarrassed, and hurt us. At least for the most part she did respect our guidance when she was in our home as a teenager. I know that you may not want to give them the satisfaction of knowing that you could ever be okay with this reunion. I know how to hurt you and the girls as well. But do we want to be right, or do we want to have a relationship with them?*

Premika, I know how stubborn you are, and I know how much Daya had to go through, the misery, the deeply distressing and disturbing experience. The terrible trauma she is still healing from. I understand what an emotional shock this must be for all of you, and I am not there to help you all through this. I ask all of you to please consider where your stubborn stance toward this relationship will lead us. Do we want to continue life without Rania? Or do we want to have a relationship with them? How about with their future children?

I am thinking of even considering sitting down with them and letting them know of the transition and how we can work through the pain, hurt, and betrayal. I think it would be best if we do let them know how difficult their relationship has been for us as parents. We should show them a support system that can help them build a strong future together. If she has been living with him for all these years, we need to accept this or we go on without her. She has accepted him and either we do too, or we don't.

If they are terrible for each other and have a rotten relationship, we can still love and support our daughter as she learns these difficult lessons. Our job as parents isn't about protecting our children from all of their bad decisions. It's letting them know they have the love and support to take risks and learn from their own mistakes.

I feel sorry for her – she does not look happy, and I may now be the only support she has in New York.

It is not a coincidence that we ran into each other. It is faith Premika. I want to continue to position myself so I can be there for her no matter the outcome. Please call when you get this letter and hopefully, we can hear each other this time.

Thinking of you and the girls always.

Love, B

This news was unexpected, and I was not sure how to handle this. Neither my parents nor us girls had any idea why she left. We were utterly perplexed. She was gone for eight years. Those years were pure hell for my mother, she cried every day. With great regrets, I have to tell you that Rania changed her mind once again and did not stay in touch with dad or any of us.

That was 30 years ago. It is only now, through being in coaching that I am finally able to understand the restrictive and abusive dynamics of our family. What my sister did, she did to save herself. I, instead, kept following through with the 'family rules' which have prevented me from becoming my own person for my entire life. I am paying a very high price for that now. In her way, my sister continues to pay, emotionally, also, because she never addressed the underlying problems with the family, she simply shifted all the blame to Veer. The anger within her is obvious and I can see it is tearing her apart. She is still living in the '80s. She cannot tolerate being in my presence. The current situation is extremely painful for me.

We were all young kids, we depended on our parents. What our parents did, the way they chose to raise us, was done out of love and good intentions, but they did it wrong. By today's standards. They had no clue that I was being abused. Now I know that if such a scenario presents itself in one's life or in the life of anyone they know, where someone is thinking of leaving everything and everyone behind, it is imperative that they seek professional help immediately. They need someone on the outside, someone non-judging to help them to figure out the dynamics in the situation that have become so extreme, that it would cause them to take this path. The sooner the problem is identified, the better the options will be, the fewer people will be hurt, and the pain will be less severe.

I do not believe anyone gets out of this kind of situation unhurt. Everyone pays some kind of emotional price. The person who left, those left behind. It is impossible to erase the past. It has happened. The past cannot be changed, and I cannot pretend it has not left some damaging impact on me. It requires work, actual therapeutic work, to become aware of the impact it has had. We all tend to repeat the patterns with which we were raised. Usually, we haven't a clue we are doing it and that is the main reason to change the inner child in us so that the pattern does not continue.

Chapter Eleven

Illegal Alien

Shortly after Rania left, we had the offer of marriage to Daya from Jason's family.

"To Daya?" Scott was more puzzled than ever. "This story is far too intriguing and keeps getting more captivating and enthralling."
Maya continued.

Oh yes, it was not me who was to be married to Jason. It was Daya's hand Jason's parents asked for in marriage. But by that time Daya was already in love with Assam, who she had met at work.

They were both working for Timer Lumber when they met. We lived in Kitty village and Assam was in central Georgetown. They fell in love. But he was Muslim, and she was Hindu, a fact that was impossible to ignore, in the small Hindu community we lived in, with a communally charged political landscape.

What followed was a dramatic love story. It even involved a mistaken accusation of elopement. In the beginning, I was the one who told many fibs to my parents, just to get Daya and Assam to see each other. I told my mom that he was my friend's boyfriend and that was why he was at every party, lion's club galas, and get-togethers we attended. I secretly used to tell my friends to invite him, so that Daya could spend time with him at the parties.

When Daya went missing, my parents first thought, was that their daughter had voluntarily eloped with the Muslim boy at work. The police immediately dragged Assam in for questioning. After Daya was found, she and Assam had to come clean about their love affair. Remember, mom and dad had accused Assam of eloping with their daughter. His parents were not happy campers either since the accusation of elopement, they had feared being arrested, given the mounting pressure from the police at the time of the abduction. Hence, Assam was afraid to talk to mom and dad about marriage, especially since he was from a different religion.

Months after Dad moved to the US, the proposal came in from Jason's parents for Daya. This devastated her and Assam. She was crying and he had gone in a recluse. After being coaxed by me and Nadia, he officially proposed. Daya confided to mom that she wanted to marry Assam. Mom was going mad in distress, wailing and weeping, saying things like "Daya how can you do this to us now?! At this time when everything that happened with Rania is finally being forgotten, and we're finally getting back into society? How can I tell my friends at mandalee that my daughter is in love with a Muslim guy? What will people say? What will people think?"

Throughout all this wailing and weeping, surprisingly, my Grandma Betsy was the calmest and most understanding. She called several times to dad and tried to convince him to turn down the proposal. Dad refused to turn it down as Jason's dad, who was his long-time friend Sal, was helping him get his documents to move to Canada. He insisted that one of us had to marry Jason. We had no choice in the matter.

Illegal Alien

After days turned into weeks without knowing what to do about the proposal from Canada, Assam and Daya came up with the idea that I could take Daya's place in the proposal.

My mom was relieved at the idea and quickly called dad to let him know we had a solution. But I profusely refused, adamant that I wanted to finish school and become a teacher.

When I told my mom, her smile disappeared and she cried, "What? Why?!" I gave her my reasons, very good ones I thought, but my mom wasn't satisfied and told me I was not allowing God to work in my life, I should just obey them and trust that God's will would be done. After all that my parents went through, there was no way they could say no and suffer any embarrassment again. They had to be able to hand over their daughter in marriage. With Dad living in the US at the time, illegal and getting immigration help from Jason's dad, Sal. How can they so no to the proposal?

After much persuading and thinking of the shame and disgrace that my parents had already been through, as well as how Daya and Assam's love would be destroyed, I relented and said yes.

The proposal was honorably welcomed by Jason's parents as soon as they saw my photo. It is that same photo on the table.

Maya pointed to one of Scott's favorite pictures of her when she was younger. She was wearing a dark green Salwar Kameez with a soft white dupatta draped over her slender shoulders. She was sitting on a small stool, her legs crossed, and her hands resting slightly over each other on her knees. On her small dainty feet, were a beautiful pair of gold and black strappy high heels sandals. Her long dark hair flowed to her waist. Her beautiful smile was one that has an almost stunning effect on others. Her eyes were breathtaking. She looked like a princess, born to enjoy all the rights and luxuries without any responsibilities.

Scott smiled as he looked over at the picture and thought to himself "no wonder they agreed. But I am now the lucky one. She's a trap set

The Ungracious Daughter

by nature, without meaning to be, a rose in which love lies in ambush! Anyone who has seen her smile has known perfection. She creates grace without movement and makes all divinity fit into her slightest gesture. Even Venus cannot compare to her." Scott's thoughts were interrupted as Maya continued.

Before the marriage, I spoke to Jason on the phone only a couple of times. We were supposed to get married in the spring of the following year, but for some unknown reason, Jason's father called and move the wedding to October of that year.

On our wedding night, we were two strangers in a room. I knew more about our watchman than my new husband. What was worse, was that I was afraid I was not a virgin - because of Khalil's abuse. I was certain that Jason would know and tell everyone, and my family would once again be disgraced. Thankfully, it was over before it started. After that night, we didn't do anything again, as we both felt like strangers, and very tired after the long rituals from our marriage ceremony.

A couple of months after marriage, I got my visa for Canada. I soon found out how different we were. He was an extrovert, I am an introvert, I had no friends, he had a ton of them. He would be on the phone most of the time, I rarely make calls and the only calls I get is from my parents. I liked staying indoors, watching movies with his mother; he like going out, partying and shopping. I still hate shopping. I like to be with my family and relatives, he spends his time with friends and hates spending time with the relatives. I like to read a lot; I don't think he even knows how. He is very lazy; I am very active.

Shortly after moving to Canada, the abuse started. That whole ordeal that I never wanted to talk about.

Dad moved to Toronto with the help from Jason's father. Mom had continuously faced difficulties in maintaining a stable life. My dad's income was lost, and although mom continued her wedding dress making business, her income from sewing classes were lost due to many raids on our home. She did not have any other means of supporting her family. My aunt advised mom to leave too. The plan was to pretend she was going to Barbados on a holiday. She would take off from Barbados to Canada, where my dad would be waiting for them. After much contemplation and debate, my mother took my aunt's suggestions and left with Nadia and Tania. I was so excited that they were coming but was disappointed that Daya could not come with them, as she was overage to be included in the sponsorship and also because she was married to Assam by then. The plans were put in place.

When they came, dad and I had already prepared for them. They were able to move to an apartment in Scarborough. Mom started to work, and Nadia and Tania went back to school. Life was good for them. We were able to get Daya and Assam to migrate to Canada only months later.

During all of my trials and tribulations with Jason, I was kept away from my family and barely knew was happening in their lives. It was approximately one year later when they finally heard from Rania again. My mother was faint with relief, over-joyed. Her emotions were on a roller coaster. My father never forgave her because she never apologized for her actions and the resulting pain, although, he too, welcomed her back and they were secretly meeting without ever knowing. I spoke to her on the phone, but I was leery, kept my emotional distance, talked with her, but never addressed the topic of why she left. I suppose I was too afraid to hear the answer.

Immediately, mom and dad went to New York to visit.

They were horrified to find out that Rania and the baby were being held at home by Veer with no permanent immigration status. She was illegal in New York City for all those years. She had just recently found out that Veer was cheating on her! With the Pandit's daughter! How quickly mom and dad forgave her for the betrayals and deceits. My dad, being a deeply religious man, said that when people withhold forgiveness or harbour resentment towards someone else, it often ends up making things worse for the person who has been wounded. He felt Rania was a wounded lamb. He compares resentment to swallowing poison and expecting the other person to die. He said when we hold onto the overwhelming emotions of anger, distress and despair, we repeatedly injure ourselves and further the damage that has been inflicted on our souls. He quickly forgave Rania for the hurt and pain and she begged them to bring her to Canada. How could they deny her a better life, after all, they blamed themselves for even introducing her to Veer in the first place. What choice did they have?

Rania told us how she got sucked in Veer's agonizing nightmare of a life filled with lies , deceit, treachery, perfidy and disloyalty. In the beginning, everything was perfect. He was this man in her life that was tender, attentive and adventurous after convincing Rania to leave the comforts of her home, her family and even her country. This thrilling man was indeed her Prince Charming.

That did not last long. After years of putting up with his lies, he was still refusing to process her application for a green card, even long after he got a divorce. She was in a dead-end job, as she had no green card and her pay was going directly to him, in his name. He had quickly become a stranger to her. They were living in a house that was giving her the creeps and she started getting night terrors and haunted dreams of really evil things. And then she started to see things. She would see a woman walking at the back of the house by the kitchen and it would freak her out, but he would calmly say it was her imagination and she was too 'light spirited.'

She was eventually rescued by the police and sent to a shelter.

She remembered getting sick at work and decided to come home. She took the train back from Manhattan to Queens and got off at Lefferts Avenue in Ozone Park, they didn't live far from the train station, so she walked the rest of the way home. It was around 10:45am. She walked past the front door and entered from the back door. She heard strange sounds coming from the bedroom. To her utter shock and dismay, she walked in on Veer and a naked woman having sex in their bed! He did not know that she was coming home early that morning as she tried to call him, but he did not pick up. What followed was a charade of screaming and yelling. Rania remembered throwing glasses and pans at him as the woman hurriedly tried to get dressed. In disbelief, she realized it was the pandit's daughter. Rania remembers screaming at him, "I hate you; you are a scumbag."

Someone must have called the police as they showed up at the door minutes later. The woman had already left. Rania was terrified as she thought she may be arrested for being illegal.

The police investigated the home as Veer clutched his bloodied arm. He tried to convince the police that it was nothing and that they could leave. The police were not buying it.

Veer asked if they were going to get arrested, as it was a big misunderstanding. Suddenly Rania retched and started to sway. She was so dizzy and fell to the ground.

The police called the ambulance. They were both taken to the hospital, as the police explained to the doctor that Rania would not say if she was hurt, but there was evidence of a fight. Just as the police were about to leave, the doctor came back in. The doctor told the police that there may be a problem, as Rania was hysterical when she came. They were about to give her something to calm her down when she told them that she may be pregnant. The doctor said she seemed confused as she did not understand how she was pregnant. Veer told her that he had a vasectomy before they met. The doctors then ran some tests and took a sonogram which confirmed that she was pregnant. Rania was puzzled because she knew she couldn't possibly get pregnant since Veer was sterile. When they told Veer, he was furious. He said it was not his. The police asked him if he thought she may have a boyfriend, maybe someone at work. He said he was not sure.

Rania was so indignant and hurt. After all, he was the one found cheating! He was the one to be blamed. Yet, here he is, telling the police that he loved her and would do anything for her. He was playing the victim! Rania was so miffed and offended.

She had been with Veer now for eight years and still did not have her green card for the US. She was illegal for all those years. Yet she could not picture her life without him, but she was not ready to go home. She told the doctors that she was afraid he may hurt her. The police knew that she was telling the truth. They sensed that Veer was trying to play the victim. That is when the Police took her to a shelter. Rania did not tell them she was illegal, no one asked about that. Rania had a lot of time to ponder on her situation now. They had never really talked about having a baby but she remembers vaguely mentioning that she wanted kids someday.

Veer had said he could not have any more children as he had a vasectomy. He had a child with his wife, and she didn't want him to father any other children. He said she forced him to get a vasectomy.

At the shelter, Veer tried to contact Rania, but all he would talk about was how she got pregnant. Rania knew it was his. After all, she had never slept with anyone else.

He was not happy and kept saying that he was not ready to be a dad again, and he didn't want anything to change between them and essentially that it would ruin what they had. To Rania's disbelief, he suggested they get rid of it. Rania knew she was not running back home again. She was keeping the baby.

Immediately after learning the results of her pregnancy test, she knew she wanted to have the baby, but she didn't want to force a child on Veer. When she was telling her story I remember her saying "ultimately it is my decision, and I thought that if I went through with terminating the pregnancy, I would regret it and resent him. On the other hand, if have it, he will resent me and the child. I felt very irresponsible and overwhelmed and that is when I knew I had to find my mother and father." That was when she made to decision that she wanted us back in life.

Mom and dad knew that Mark and Jason knew someone who could help, so we decided to bring her by boat to Center Island, in Toronto. From there, Jason and I picked her up and my parents took her home.

Mark had a friend, a veteran immigration officer, who used to be stationed at the US-Canadian Border Patrol Station, located in Niagara Falls. He was now the smuggler of illegal aliens. They called him "Red Man." The plans were in place for the next move. It was a stormy night with gusts of violent winds and the treacherous rain.

Later that evening Rania told us the entire ordeal.

Rania recalled that she looked at the map in her hand and was happy. It was the map of Canada, a place she only saw in movies. A place where her family now resided. She remembered walking over to the waterfront and reflecting on her surroundings. She was observing the faces of the people that would travel with her to an unknown destination. She was hoping it would have been just her, but in her illegal situation, she had to take what she could get, as this was a promise for a better life. The immigrants were men, women, young adult girls, and boys. However, their faces didn't reflect their youth. A few of the illegal immigrants were laughing and a few were saying prayers. They were all praying for a better life in Canada after being in America illegally for so long. Rania looked behind her to see the lights of Manhattan city from far away. She recalled taking a deep breath and closing her eyes for a few seconds. The thought of seeing her sisters again filled her lungs with oxygen. She had not seen us for so many years now. Those memories encouraged her tendency to feel happy.

A low voice was heard from far away. She looked over and saw "Red Man" and Mark, the man responsible for all the illegal immigration, coming toward her. She vaguely remembers Mark from back home, when our parents visited Jason's parents, but that was a long time ago. He did not look the same. His boyish good looks were now more manly and valiant. Mark promised Rania and the others they would travel from New York to Canada. However, none of the illegal immigrants knew where they would settle in Canada, they were all driven by their faith. The faith in a better future.

"Is everyone ready? There is no time for any hesitation or tears. It is time that you understand the regulations. We already went over them, and I don't need to repeat myself."
Doubts and questions were filling Rania's mind as she listened to the lecture about the safety and the risks of this trip.
Then Mark came near her. He stood a few steps away and studied Rania for a few seconds. Rania was looking at her reflection on a broken mirror buried in the sand.
"Don't worry, everything will be fine," Mark assured her. He too seems to remember her from back home
"Do you think that we will make it?" Rania had asked him.
"Sure, we will. Don't you believe?"

The fibreglass boat idled on the darkened Lake Ontario a few miles south of American waters. It was roughly 25 feet long and seven feet wide, unlit, overloaded and offering no shelter from the elements. A loud sound was heard from far away that signalled their boarding. The others started to fill a boat made for one hundred passengers. Most of these immigrants can't swim and most of them only spoke Guyanese English. However, they all had faith that this one step could change their families' lives. Men, women and children all crammed aboard. Most were seated on narrow benches. A few huddled on the vomit-splattered deck. Some had opened slits in plastic garbage bags and pushed heads and arms through, flimsy protection against the damp night chill. Few life jackets were visible. At the boat's stern, two Guyanese Americans tended a 200-horsepower outboard engine and 10 plastic barrels of fuel. They were in the final hour of ferrying a load of undocumented migrants toward Centre Island, in waters nearly three-quarters of a mile deep. Human smugglers, running a boat through a seam where black water met the black sky. The Toronto Centre Islands are located just offshore from the city's downtown area and have a chain of 15 small islands in Lake Ontario, south of mainland Toronto. They had to go through 1000 islands first. They were headed for Frenchman's Bay in Pickering, not Toronto mainland, as Rania had assumed.

It started to rain, and the power of the wind was increasing. The boats started to rock back and forth on the surface of the water. Rania said it was cold and she had to shove her hands in her coat pockets after she had tightly covered her mouth from the cold winds. The glistening water looked like it was hugging the boat like a mother who's putting her child to sleep.

The boat operators, one a former commercial fisherman and the other his cousin, had picked up their passengers earlier in the night on a beach on the Manhattan coastline and worked their way offshore towards Lake Ontario.

The bright Toronto lights twinkled in the distance. The boat's destination was the steep outcropping of Frenchman's, beside the entrance wharf street marina, where the men running the boat had been told a pickup crew and would guide them to the beach with a flashing light. From there the migrants were expected to follow the usual human-smuggling routine — a leap into the surf, a scramble ashore, a rush to waiting vehicles, a drive to safe houses where they would be held until the balance of their smuggling fees had been paid. And then, if it all worked, if no one drowned, Toronto or Durham law-enforcement agencies did not catch them, they would embark on a furtive form of opportunity in Canada. On the Sandy beaches of Frenchman's Bay, Jason and I watched as several people got off the boat, after crossing the lake and climbing the bank before disappearing among the trees on the other side of the beach.

They came from multiple American states and matched familiar profiles of undocumented migrants seeking to cross. For Rania, she was journeying home. Her tears were unseen for they had blended in with the rain.

The Ungracious Daughter

Rania lifted her bag and walked toward Jason and I. She wanted the Canadian dream. She wanted to come to Canada to live with her family, to live with us on day one. When we got home, she went straight to the washroom and started crying, she never thought she would ever do something like that.

Maya ended her story of Rania that day. Years later, due to their disputes and conflicts, Rania and Maya would become estranged, causing Maya to wonder whether Rania was really the Ungracious Daughter after all.

Chapter Twelve

The Rogue

Weeks after Maya told her story, they were busy planning their first vacation to Mexico, when out nowhere, Dinesh started calling Nadia, threatening that he would make sure Maya's relationship with Scott never last and that he would go to Scott's house to tell him that Maya was still seeing him. Nadia was flabbergasted to find out that he knew where Scott lived, worked and what he drove! Nadia invited Scott and Maya over for dinner to warn them of Dinesh's threats.

Scott knew that Maya had moved on from Rahul. After many years of being alone, she briefly started a relationship with Dinesh, but it ended as quickly as it started. It became apparent to Maya that he was a narcissist and was gas lighting all the while.

As told by Nadia to Scott

The Ungracious Daughter

With Jason, Maya was trapped in a marriage that was sexually, physically, emotionally, mentally, and financially abusive.

With Rahul, it was psychological and emotional abuse. Then, sadly, we watched as she ended with a psychotic narcissist, the Rogue Dinesh. It was as if she would never find "her person." She was in a vicious cycle of unhealthy relationships, and we watched helplessly as she was treated like a doormat over and over again, by this egotistical narcissist. We watched as once again as her self-esteem and confidence were robbed from her as he controlled and manipulated her.

When they met, things were great. Maya was living with her four children, in a beautiful townhouse in Ajax. We were all so proud of how she singlehandedly renovated that old townhouse to look like a brand-new modern home. It was small townhouse, yet we saw how happy and content the children were, even after leaving the comfort and luxury of big house in Pickering. They were such a happy family. After the fiasco with Rahul, we were all so concerned about her, but Maya delved into work, volunteering and taking care of her children. Although she had to go to court almost every Friday, fighting two custody battles with Jason and his father, she stayed strong and raised four wonderful children.

After some months of dating, Dinesh started sleeping over when the older kids went to visit their grandparents. He would bring his daughter, who was a year younger than Sean. They would play together and got along nicely. It was nice to see Maya dating again and she seemed happy. But I must say, our mother did not like Dinesh one bit. From the beginning she saw right through him. When he moved in with Maya, we were all horrified.

Several weeks after living with Maya and the kids, he started hinting that they should move closer to the kid's grandparents so that they could walk over to see them whenever they wanted to. When Maya told me, I instantly thought to myself, "she does not realize that she is being played, he was playing mind games with her, manipulating her, using her bond with her kids to get to her emotions and get what he wants. She was *not seeing it and she started to detach herself from us when we tried to talk to her about it. We were helpless."*

Maya continued as Nadia stopped, picking up from where Nadia could not carry on.

It is true, I wanted to do this on my own, to make my own decisions, and live by them no matter what. I thought moving closer to the grandparents was a great idea. We bought a massive house in Pickering so that each of the children, including his daughter, could have their own bedroom, just a street away from my children's grandparents.

The plan was for me to use the money from the sale of the townhouse, and he would match it, even if he had to borrow from his brother, so we could have a substantial down payment.

On the day the down payment was due, he announced that he didn't have enough money for the down payment and that his brother could not lend. So, I used all of the profits from the sale of the townhouse so we can reach the amount for the down payment. I had made a substantial profit on the sale.

It was very frustrating and exasperating, and I kept asking if he had money in his bank and he kept reassuring me that he did. The evening of our move to the new house, as soon as we were almost complete, he discovered he knew someone on the street, so he went over to say hello. His brothers had been helping with the move and took a break to have a beer. As I handed the older one a beer, his words made me freeze. He said "So I guess mom and Carrie allowed Dinesh to use his money after all to buy this big house. He looked around the large living room and commented "I am sure you can't pay for this on your own."

I could not believe my ears. That bastard made me use all my money from the sale of the townhouse because he knew it was a significant amount.

From that day on, things changed. And that was the first day in our beautiful new home. His behaviour change was obvious and so was mine. I felt the trust was gone. He used to help me to cook and take care of the kids when we were in the townhouse, but all that stopped when we moved.

He used to get home from work at 5:30 pm but was now regularly coming home at 7:00 pm, claiming he had to work.

There was a big lag in communication, as he won't talk, claiming he was too tired from work and was always deflecting and changing the subject. When I asked for any kind of communication, we would end up fighting.

He took me by surprise when he suddenly announced that he was the youngest son, and traditionally his parents had to come to live with us. This announcement caused more frustrations for me, endless arguments and quarrels ensued as he started coming home later and later. He was spending more and more time at his sister's house, where his parents lived, insisting that his parents needed him.

Daily he would persuade and coax me, convincing me that if his mother was living with us, she would cook, clean and take care of Sean so we didn't have to pay for daycare, and that if we got married, our finances would be combined, and we would be set for life. Eventually, I relented to both the marriage and allowed his parents to move in with us.

We ended up making our living quarters in the basement, and gave his mother the master bedroom. Shockingly, she refused to share a room with her husband, demanding that he had to get his own room since she had not slept with him since Dinesh was born. Ryder, unwillingly, had to share a room with his daughter, Natasha.

Things worsened, even after shifting to these intolerable living arrangements. His mother downright refused to cook or take care of Sean, who was in half-day kindergarten at the time. Her words were "I will only take care of my own grandchildren. No one else." She took care of Natasha, but we had to take Sean to half-day care.

The Rogue

When Dinesh first told his mother that he wanted to marry me — an older woman with four children, as she pointed out frequently, it was as if an apocalypse hit the house. His mother took ill and was in bed for days. Every conversation was a flurry of tears, recriminations, bargaining, and desperate demands to overturn the unacceptable, wildly reckless decision he was taking, of marrying an 'old woman with four pickneys,' according to her.

Seeing her like this and hearing her words or ridicule and scorn for me, I knew that I could not live with her, or with Dinesh any longer. I would not let my children see me as weak and insubstantial. I could not marry this man or be in this family.

I felt stifled, smothered as if I was suffocating. I was fighting for that connection I had with Dinesh when we were living in the townhouse. I could not find it. We were on daily rounds of arguments and quarrels. I was again fighting to be seen and heard. I know from my experience that I should never have to fight for a relationship. Fighting to stay or fighting to leave. I had done all that already. I had fought to be loved and respected. I fought for my children. I fought for their future. I fought for my own future.

I knew that eventually, the fighting had to stop. I had enough. He could not fight by himself. I became aware of my responses, and it signalled the beginning of my plans to leave. I was far beyond caring as I had become too emotionally detached by then. I did not want to fight for him. I know that if I did, I would completely lose touch with myself and be lost in him again. He did not seem to care either. I felt lonely, confused and miserable. It was a hopeless place to reside. My gut wisdom was telling me that all he wanted was the house. He was more concerned about who was getting the house when we split than saving the relationship. And I could not turn to my family. I had disassociated from them to be with him. They had warned me so many times about him. My mother forewarned me that he saw what I had and wanted it, my home, my new minivan, my stable job. He wanted a ticket to financial freedom, and I was his path of getting there.

After bouts of verbal abuse, lies, false promises, and manipulation, he would then pretend nothing had happened, returning with sweet words, flowers at work, texts of apology, playing the victim, appealing to my empathic nature. All pre-planned and geared to derail and torment me.

As children growing up in Guyana and West Indian homes, we were taught to be silent, "speak when spoken to, be seen and not heard." West Indians know those words very well. So, I kept my mouth shut all those years, with Jason and then Rahul. But not anymore.

I was very open, raw, and vulnerable with my traumas and false beliefs about myself. This Narcissist played to my weaknesses. He also used these tools to his advantage. He used to blame me, constantly gaslighting, and manipulating me, and displayed his arrogance and ignorance like a badge of honour.

He would tell me things like "who would want you with four children." He would tell me I was crazy, that I had bipolar disorder, that I was horrible, dissatisfied.
He would say things like, I could never be happy, that I had too high of expectations, that I was a perfectionist, that I had OCD, that I created my own problems.

But the last blow of his wickedness was yet to come.

Maya paused, as Nadia poured another glass of Jacob's Creek Rose Moscato. It was their favourite. Scott and Nadia's husband, Shawn, were drinking Guyana's El Dorado 15-year Rum. They too poured another as Maya continued. Shawn smiling at Nadia, as he knew the strange tale was coming next. They had heard this weird story before. Shawn, not believing in Obeah, was amused at this story and thought, that although it was bizarre, there has to be another logical explanation.

Phantastic

I do not believe in Obeah, evil or wrongdoings, or any kind of sorcery. Obeah is a kind of sorcery or witchcraft, practiced especially in the Caribbean. Anyway, one faithful night, something very bizarre happened.

Scott looked at both Maya and Nadia in disbelief, thinking they must be joking. But they both looked serious as Maya continued.

I was in the basement reading, and Dinesh was in the shower. He takes forever in the shower. When he does take a shower, which was not very often. I looked up and I noticed on his dresser, he had a small book. It was very old, torn and worn and had almost a cloth-like cover. It was sitting amongst some other books. The only reason I noticed it was it had a bright yellow sticky note jutting out of it. I thought to myself "wow he's reading!" He does not read.

Curiosity got the better of me and so I got up and went over to pick up the book. I opened it to the page that had the sticky note. In disbelief and shock, I read line after line. It was instructions on a mantra, which is a powerful ancient spiritual practice, on how to make someone fall in love with you and stay in love with you. I read it over and over. The mantra I don't remember clearly, but the instructions read:

> *Say this mantra three times, squeeze the juices of a white flower into a clear liquid, like water, juice or clear alcohol, as you read the mantra. Then give the glass of water, juice or alcohol to the person you want to fall in love with you. The person must take the drink from you with his/her own hands. This mantra can be used many times and on multiple persons.*

This struck me like a bolt of lightning. I read the mantra, again and again, and an uncanny feeling came over me. He had been doing this to me, was my immediate thought!

I used to notice that he would buy white carnations and leave them in the fridge. I did ask him once about all these white carnations he bought, and he said that his mom did "Lord Shiva puja," and this requires white flowers. I know this to be true, so I never paid any more attention to it, but as I read these instructions about this flower in the drink, I was horrified and shocked. Moments of him giving me a clear drink flashed before me. Most weekends, after watching movies and putting the children to bed, we would head downstairs to our quarters, and he would insist we have a drink or two to unwind. He would say things like "go shower and relax, I'll make us a drink." It was always vodka and Perrier water. I started to think, maybe he did this ritual every time he made the drinks for me!

I put the book back where it was and for the first time, I felt disgusted by him. I looked at him and thought, what the heck am I doing with this man? Why am I letting him treat me like this? Why am I living in the basement of my own home? To be honest, at that moment, my thoughts were racing, how badly he treated me. I couldn't understand what I was doing with him. Why was I allowing him to treat me like this? I even allowed him to let people at the temple believe that we were not together. We would go to temple in separate cars, me with my children and him, with his mother and daughter. He wanted people to believe that he was single. And I allowed him to do this!

From that day on, I started to loathe him. I started to detest his little snide remarks, belittling me and my children. I couldn't breathe, I wasn't eating or sleeping. I had debilitating back pain, brain fog, stress and anxiety.

I knew that I no longer wanted to be with him. It was close to Christmas, and I had already bought him a nice warm coat for Christmas, and he was wearing a light jacket throughout the winter, not wanting to spend money. The following week, I left the coat in the garage, and told him that it was over. He didn't believe me at first. He ignored me. He knew that every time I said such things, he would beg me, and I would relent and surrender to his bidding. But this time was different from the other times, it was the end of an era for me.

That moment of clarity when I decided to leave, was a moment of revelation. I had put much effort into learning to love myself and I knew that I could not go down that path again. Just because he chose not to fight for me, doesn't mean I am not good enough a person.

I was ready to release the shackles. My worth was not in his hands. I had to stand up and fight for myself. To redeem me. It was the only way out of the dark hole. I knew that I had value, self-compassion, self-acceptance and self-respect. Fighting for myself was far easier than fighting a losing battle with someone who doesn't know how to love me the way I deserved to be loved. The reason I had stayed trapped for so long was that I chose to ignore my gut wisdom. Now I knew I had to build back from my childhood. I had to build myself to trust myself and believe in my intuition and listen to my intuition. I knew I had to get out because I kept repeating the same cycles of finding the same type of men. And that was because I felt I was not worthy enough for anything better.

I needed to leave to survive. I had become so anxious again, the same cycle repeating itself. I couldn't breathe. I felt as if I was suffocating. I had debilitating back pain, brain fog, zero motivation, and a dread of the future. A future that I need to start rebuilding once again.

The realization that I was repeating the same patterns of allowing men to ruin me. I allowed Khalil to abuse and manipulate me, I allowed myself to stay with Jason the narcissist and rapist, and I chose to be with Rahul, who was a cheat, liar and manipulator. And here I am again, with Dinesh, the narcissistic psychopath, the gas lighter.

I felt so very angry at myself. I felt so deeply wounded and angry, with the universe, with God, with life. Life is so unfair. At this stage in my life, I should be on route to achieving what I set out to achieve. This heart-wrenching pain came with the realization that I had made yet another horrible mistake. The brutal suffering of my soul was unbearable.

The factual realization that Dinesh used me, that he saw an opportunity to easily get what he wanted, without much effort. He saw how vulnerable I was, he saw that I only needed to be shown a little love and I was happy.

He saw that I was already established in my life, he saw the beautiful fully furnished home I had, the new minivan, and a well-established career. I was good financially. It was easy for him. He just had to walk in and take it.

Maya stopped just as Nadia announced dinner was ready. She had made roasted lamb, potatoes and steamed greens. The table was laid nicely with turquoise linen and white and silver placemats. Nadia always outclassed everyone in the family with her table settings. Her boys, Zack and Nathan, came down from their rooms to have dinner with them. Maya was their favorite aunt and they loved Scott the moment they met him. Yet, today, they knew after dinner they had to return to their rooms as the adults had a serious family discussion ahead of them.

Chapter Thirteen

Living My Best Life

Maya helped the boys and Nadia clear the table and put the dishes in the dishwasher. After dessert of sponge cake and ice cream, Maya continued.

Once again, I left with not much money in my bank, but with my strong gut wisdom, with my voice. I was looking out for my beautiful children. I know that if I trust myself, everything will be okay.

I had to reframe my inner child. I had to start there and work my way back to me, who I was today and why.

I knew I had to go back to my childhood. I had to rebuild myself, trust myself, believe in my intuition and listen to my gut wisdom. I had very bad relationships with narcissistic partners, and I knew that I had to get out of repeating the same cycles, of finding the same type of man.

The Ungracious Daughter

I had to open my 'third eye" and reframe my mind to work through the traumas and false beliefs about myself. In Hinduism, the third eye symbolizes a higher state of consciousness through which you can perceive the world. Using traditional meditation techniques, you can open up this chakra and gain a deeper, more enlightened understanding of the universe around you. My grandfather had taught us this when we were younger.

I give myself the freedom to speak, to use that inner voice, that voice that is also known as my intuition. To this day, it has remained my loyal and trusted companion. It speaks to me with brutal honesty the reason. In my past relationships, I chose to ignore that voice of reason, that gut intuition for far too long. That intuition, that gut wisdom, I call "The Voice," has given me my key to freedom. It has remained my loyal and trusted companion ever since. It speaks to me with brutal honesty.

It took several years but eventually, I was able to buy a home gain, raising four children alone, doing whatever I could to support us financially, emotionally, and physically, including having a full-time managerial job, running the dance school, wedding business and decorating business, all while getting no financial help from Jason or Rahul.

I did it all for my children. I also wanted to be the proof to others like me that there is a light outside of your darkness, that you could find a way because in this lifetime you deserve all that you desire.

As I started working on myself, I discovered something about myself. My pattern is the need for validation, praise, recognition, and acceptance. So, despite all of Dinesh's emotional manipulation, the moment he displayed words or acts that made me feel wanted and needed, I craved it. I lapped up the compliments like a cat devouring cream. I was very good at forgiveness, and I was an expert at ignoring the bad when the good landed on my lap. I knew I had to go through my hardships, the abuse, the pain, the suffering. I had to learn to handle it, to deal with the pain, and the shame so that I could empower myself and help other women who are not able to do this on their own.

I had to be that support, for myself and for them. There was no other way to learn what I have learned if I didn't go through all that.

I have to keep my own counsel, my direction with only the influence of the divine. I know that there must come a time, a day, a moment when I get to say I've done what I set out to do.

Now, I can have your love, because your influence at that point, is a bonus, a boost, a benefit to whatever comes next. Yet for now. At this moment. I am so happy to be loved by you.

We cannot undo these abuses but talking about these issues and spreading awareness might help people prevent such actions. We need to understand that children who face emotional abuse still bears those marks as adults which affect their lives along with those of their peers too.

I have chosen to step up. For all those women and girls who cannot. It is time to speak up and shout out, to be the voice for millions of others who cannot put into words or understand the depths of their suffering.

It is my goal that speaking will allow others to understand why it is my calling to come forward. To help others to recognize abuse and escape. To recover from sexual, physical, financial and emotional abuse. It is my mission, my passion, and my purpose to show others how to transform pain into power. I was trapped in a physically, emotionally, mentally, financially abusive marriage followed by another emotionally abusive one. But I stayed strong and found the courage to escape.

These small self-care practices began to gain momentum until I reached a tipping point. I'm no longer pulled into the downward spiral of despair. Instead, what happened fuels my desire to be even kinder to myself, and to spread this information to others who are suffering from abuse. My self-care practices are what let me believe that I am worthy of true love, and not to give up on me, my mission now is to provide relief and understanding to women like me who have suffered so that they too can live their best life.

This was a fate. I was determined to break free from this cycle, this pattern. I saw the future, I knew I was not going to follow this same route again. I knew then that I deserve better, I knew then that I deserved to be loved, the real thing.

Scott laughed, and hugged Maya, remembering that was Maya's profile name on Match.com

Maya smiled pulled Scott closer to her and continued.

I know I have the voice for the voiceless, I know I had to be strong and courageous to give other women some hope.

I trusted that my intuition, my gut wisdom, for the foreseeable path. It was already pre-laid; I just need the courage to step one foot onto it.

I threw myself into full-time healing and self-development, focusing on the inner child, family patterns and conditioning, and my lack of self-worth that kept me stuck for years.

But I was on a path of healing; I could take a full breath and my back pain started to fade. This physical transformation blew me away. Within two weeks my face changed. My eyes started to sparkle again, and my smile returned (not the fake one I had practiced so well), and I felt a sense of relief and freedom that gave me. A new lease on life.

I was stopped by people in the mandir asking 'what's your secret to looking ten years younger?' My transformation was noticeable to others.

It is throughout my journey from the abyss of suffering to ultimate freedom that I hope to inspire others. What I have learned throughout my healing is that relationship co-creation was something I needed to take full responsibility for. And if I didn't deconstruct my patterns and the reasons why I attracted him in the first place, I would never break this narcissistic/empath dance.

Not only that, but I also have four beautiful children, and my self-healing was a gift to them, otherwise, their destiny would be in meeting a narcissistic partner. This is how generational patterns work. It's fascinating.

My journey began from the ground upwards, peeling back the onion layers of what was my trauma bonding and codependency. I am enjoying having found myself again - my true self.

It is in the understanding of our patterns and limiting beliefs that we find out who we truly are, underneath the falseness of what's playing out with us. Partner, family, children, friends, boss, the list goes on.

Now I am brave, beautiful, and worthy. I know that deserve better; it is my time to walk the path to freedom and joy.

Love and light

Scott's words

I hope talking about this will help you understand yourself better. Even if just getting out, speaking about it, and not keeping the secrets anymore will help you to sleep better at night. You have my love always, no matter what comes from this. My wishes are that your nightmares will stop, and you will be able to give voice to the voiceless, strength to the weak, courage to the meek, and be brave for the fearful ones.

The Voice

Years later, as I was trying to get my life back and started my six self-care rituals of getting proper sleep, drinking more water, ensuring proper nutrition for both me and the children, incorporating exercise and movement in our lives. I joined the gym and added a women's dance class to my dance school services. I enrolled the boys in basketball training and the girls were in dance with me. We started enjoying nature by going on weekly picnics. I ensured that I had a strong social connection with friends and family, as well as many people from the temple, who have now become like family to me. Opening, talking, being vulnerable, being heard, hearing a different perspective, laughing, and receiving empathy had become so beneficial to me. I felt that my shared sorrow was halved, and my shared joy is doubled. I started gardening and journaling as well.

I believe that it is my destiny to come forward and help others to recognize, escape and recover from sexual, domestic, emotional, financial, emotional, and physical abuse. It is my mission, my passion, and my purpose to express to others how to transform their pain into power and positivity.

Maya and Scott bade farewell to Nadia and Shawn. Maya felt a sense of relief. She was happy that she was able to share so much with Scott and her family and talk about her past. She felt blessed for the support in her emotional healing. She had released an enormous number of emotions and imbalances in her body since she started sharing her story with Scott, letting go of all the pent-up emotions, hurt, guilt, fear and shame.

As a survivor, she came to forgive Khalil for most of it. The tremendous relaxation that she felt afterward was exuberant. She felt like a ton of bricks had been lifted off of her shoulders. She felt liberated that she was able to share even the heavy facts of her life with Scott.

It did not matter if she was the Ungracious Daughter or not. Now she was ready to love Scott without borders.

The end

Sandy Maeck, R.C.M, O.L.C.M

Author, Health and Life Coach - Toronto

Sandy Maeck is a Toronto-based Author, Life & Health Coach. Her journey and track record of turning adversity into opportunities are sure to make you feel inspired. Which is what drives her career as a coach. Her journey is very similar to that of her books "The Unwanted Wife" and "The Ungracious Daughter".

She is also a licenced Condominium property manager with two accredited licences.

Sandy is a survivor of Domestic Violence and Sexual Abuse. She migrated to Canada in 1985 due to an arranged marriage. Although she had a passion for writing and dancing, her life did not allow her that luxury. Amongst the struggles of being a single mother of four children and facing hardships in failed marriages, Sandy worked as a leader in the business industry. She is also the founder and Artistic Director of STCC Dance Academy and Owner and Director of Shobha's Wedding Services.

While she worked through profound challenges in her own life, she also found ways to help empower others. Since then, Sandy uses her strength and knowledge to help people achieve their unique version of personal success and empowerment.

Sandy has always been highly motivated, as well as super motivational. Her spirit and her energy is infectious.

Most notably, she has a long-standing history of excellence and has received several awards of recognition for her achievements and outstanding volunteer work. She leads with passion and strength to overcome challenges, and inspires everyone around her along the way.

Sandy has found both a balance and a life rhythm, which she has devoted herself to coaching and sharing with those who are searching for the same.

As an inspirational speaker, Sandy engages in the following topics:
1. Surviving Domestic Violence and Abuse
2. Empowerment After Domestic Violence and Abuse; and
3. Health and Lifestyle Changes

She can also create custom talks to powerfully connect with any audience.

Sandy is a strong advocate against domestic violence and abuse. She provides consultations for women who feel lost and are dealing with domestic trauma. She is also a strong advocate for living a healthy lifestyle.

If interested, to inquire about Sandy's services or to book her to speak at your event(s), please contact her by phone at (416) 722-3998 or by email at sandy@sandymaeck.com
Or visit:
www.sandymaeck.com